# THE JIGSAW ME
## BUILDING BALANCE

## INTO YOUR DIET WITH
## THE POWER OF THE
## MOON

Alison Marsden

# The Jigsaw Method

# Contents

# Legal Bit

# Dedication

I dedicate this book to all my past clients without whom this book would not have been written.

And to all my future clients, without you I would not have taken the long journey to get it published and make the world of changing your diet a friendlier place.

Also, to my Dad, who succumbed to bowel cancer and dementia, and has passed on to other realms. He helped me to have the perseverance to keep going.

# Preface

*How can you change something that does not exist?*

Are you feeling overwhelmed and frustrated by conflicting diet advice? Are you struggling with physical symptoms such as bloating, brain fog, or low energy that you suspect might be related to your food choices? Are you looking for a more holistic approach to food that considers your overall health and wellbeing, and helps you find balance? If so, read on to learn more about a programme that could be the solution you've been seeking.

Imagine finding a simple, food-based solution to your health concerns, rather than relying on supplements or medication that can cause additional problems. Imagine feeling in tune with your body and instinctively choosing the foods that support your health and balance. This programme can help you establish a healthy, sustainable dietary routine that resets your digestion and brings your body and mind into harmony.

Perhaps the biggest challenge to changing your diet is finding the time and energy to do it, especially if you have a busy schedule or a set routine that feels hard to break. That's why this process starts small, with just one meal a week, and gradually builds up to a full 24 hours. And it incorporates an easy, effortless way to make changes to your diet, some of which require no new recipes or ingredients, by simply aligning your meals with the phases of the moon and your body's internal organs.

But will this approach make a difference to your specific health issues, such as abdominal pain, anxiety, brain fog, or skin problems? As a holistic system that addresses all aspects of your health, the Jigsaw Method has the potential to bring a wide range of conditions back into balance. By starting with the edges and corners of the puzzle, as it were, you'll find that all the other pieces fall into place naturally.

# Foreword

I was first introduced to Alison Marsden during 2020, a year that brought many challenges to maintaining physical and mental wellbeing. Shortly before the pandemic struck, I was diagnosed with cancer; this led me to christen that year my 'candemic'.

So many of us had to make significant changes to our lifestyles; but something else happened. We started to question the quality of our lifestyles and food we had been eating up to that point. I am excited that so many people will benefit from Alison's book, and I felt honoured when Alison invited me to write a foreword to her ground-breaking approach. I believe the Rebalance Diet will have a huge, positive impact on the world. Having tried various health regimes in the past, and being now confronted with very specific health and recovery challenges, I knew it was time to find an approach that encompassed overall and lifelong wellbeing.

When I first met Alison at a networking event, I was struck by her quiet commitment to the benefits of the Alexander technique. After my operation, and having been sent on my way with a leaflet on post-surgery exercises, I booked several sessions with Alison. As I began to live out the choices about how I moved physically and being released from old and unhelpful ways of thinking, this mindset led me to making calmer and better choices in other areas of my life. It then felt like a natural progression for me to learn about Alison's Rebalancing Your Diet with Bio-dynamic Lifestyle approach.

From the outset, Alison explains the evolution of the Rebalance process and the ideas upon which it is based. The key principles of this approach, which made sense to both my mind and body, are to rest my ingestion period for one day per week, timing certain food and water to be eaten at set times and to rebalance my diet according to seasonal food. The result is that you feel the change within your body. Free from the distractions caused by an imbalanced digestive system, we can think more clearly, more steadily, and in a calmer way. This programme resynchronises our diet with our natural biorhythms. Tensions are released and life starts to flow more easily.

Daily critical times are recommended for certain foods when each organ is most active. I found this worked well and particularly for water. I realised that I was experiencing something of an energy slump around 3–4 pm and assumed it was hunger. By simply upping my water intake at this time, and maybe eating a few pumpkin seeds, my hunger remains at bay until it's time for my evening meal. The diet leans towards a slow release of energy. I tend to do things in bursts and then get tired, and it helps me to manage this pattern better.

I know that Alison has carefully and lovingly created her recipes using home-grown, organic and fresh foods, some in combinations that I haven't come across anywhere else. Of course, taste and texture are equally important, and I can assure you that all of Alison's recipes are absolutely delicious! I love that nothing is wasted and tell all my family and friends how to make Alison's stock, rich in potassium and other vitamins and minerals, always available in my fridge and consistently drawing compliments when used as a base for family meals.

I have followed various other diets and plans but they are neither sustainable nor desirable in the long term. Alison's Rebalance diet has helped me see that by working with our natural rhythms, we can refine both what we eat and when. It just feels right and gets easier and easier, leaving your mind and body in better shape and grateful!

Alison's Rebalance diet is unique and yummy. I wish you well as you embark on your path to better health and wellbeing.

Coralie Hobson

# Acknowledgements

I wish to thank all these people that have helped me in some way to write this book.

Elaine Hale, who gave me that first step of realising I was *not* the only one! Christine Armstrong, who gave me such creative ideas on the seasons. Hazel Macfarlane, who got me to take that first step to get it published.

My sister Helen, who gave me that first steppingstone to let someone else see it in its whole. My first proofreader Rachel Gritswood, who let me open up to the fact I was dyslexic. To my herbalist Julia Russell, who opened my eyes to detoxing organs. To my clients, who were happy to use their records as my success stories.

And finally, my business mentors who gave me the energy and vision to do it!

# Who this Book Is Intended For

Here are *some* examples of people who could find this book helpful:

People who are **over 40** where their digestive enzymes and food requirements have *reduced* and who would like to rebalance the amount of food that they eat to maintain a healthy weight.

Mothers who have stopped breastfeeding, or who are at the tail end of breastfeeding, and wish to move away from any 'grazing' habits to get their diet back on track without too much effort.

People who would like to get their **weight back into balance** and would like a different structure to use other than *counting calories*.

People who are interested in rebalancing their gut's **microflora** due to symptoms of excessive bloating and discomfort in their abdomen.

People with **auto-immune conditions** who wish to address their condition through diet. There are lots of books out there that explain how diet can be the *cause* of their auto-immune condition, but do not always offer help on *how* to carry out these dietary changes. This book is about *how to implement* the changes in your diet gradually, step by step, helping you see progress and purpose in your journey to change your diet and improve your health.

**Menopausal women**. This phase in life is often about a *clearing out* and this book offers a *gentle* approach to this process.

**Type 2 diabetics** who would like to rebalance blood sugar levels without the use of drugs. Please consult your GP before you follow this book if you are currently on medication.

Here are some examples of who this book is *not* intended for:

People who suffer from eating disorders such as **anorexia nervosa** or **bulimia nervosa**. In these cases, it *may be* more advisable to look at methods to *nurture* themselves (rather than making changes to their diet). In *some* instances, people with these conditions, may need help to be reassured that they *deserve* to be nurtured. Sometimes the cause of these conditions is more about a *control* issue. In this case they could practise techniques such as Yoga, the Alexander Technique, talking therapies, the Feldenkrais Method etc. to help bring anxiety or any other challenging emotion under control, which *may* otherwise lead them to an *extreme* desire to control their diet.

**Pregnant women**. Often during this phase women need to *graze* to be able to fulfil all their nutritional needs due to the size of the baby and issues such as morning sickness. In these cases, pregnant women really need to eat whatever they feel like when they get the desire to eat.

**Young children** who may need at least three meals *every day* to obtain their nutritional needs.

# Introduction

# Finding Balance through a Holistic Approach to Food

One day while I was driving my six-year-old son to school, he asked, 'Mum, if you could breathe **in** but you could not breathe *out* would you survive?' The answer was obvious, and I proceeded to explain to him why you could not possibly survive. As I did, I realised that this is happening to many people but with regard to food. Our culture has lost the balance between the ingestion (breathing in) and the elimination phase (breathing out). This is now causing us many different illnesses. However, it is a slow and hidden process and people just do not realise that this could be the cause of their ill health.

## The Mind–Body Process of Changing Your Diet

My main profession is not that of nutritionist but an Alexander Technique teacher; this is someone who teaches people a mind–body process to help change habits. One of the biggest hurdles is realising our sensory perception: what we think we are receiving through our sensory system, is not always what is **actually** happening.

## Our Unreliable Sensory Perception

As I read my book in bed, winding down from the day, I put an eye patch over one eye and read with a torch with the other. The eye with the patch on develops night vision and the reading eye's pupil is reduced to accommodate the bright light from the torch. When I am ready to fall asleep, I turn the torch off and remove the eye patch. I then see just darkness with the eye that has been reading but the eye which had the eye patch on, **has** the night vision and gives me a view of the room even in darkness. However, and this is the main point, I also get a **stimulus** on the skin round my eye that has been reading that **feels** as if I now have an eye patch on as I cannot see anything with this eye! When I first did this, I put my hand on that eye to remove what I thought was the 'eye patch' as the stimulus was that strong! Our sensory system can stimulate our nervous system (and our hormonal system). It is amazing what we really do sense, and raises the question, 'what is reality?'

## How We Can Learn a More Reliable Sensory Perception with Food

In order for us to see what is **really** happening with our diets we need to **rest** the ingestion phase. This is very challenging in our hectic lifestyles and our toxic environment. But we can do it **gradually**, and we can do it with the support of our **biorhythms**. This is what the **Rebalance** day is all about, a 24-hour period just **once** a week, where you reduce and minimise the ingestion phase and connect to your body's biorhythms. When we start to see the positive effects and have a programme of progression and purpose, we then get the **motivation** and **perseverance** to continue on this journey of improved health. Not only can some health conditions begin to subside, but our energy and vitality can start to increase, with a balanced immune system. We then begin to finally breathe out with respect to our digestion.

What constitutes healthy food is a big debate, however, after reading this book you will be equipped with a sort of **'compass'** to navigate through the **maze** of which foods to eat: a rescue guide to help you through the hurdles: and a progress plan to help you maintain **purpose** and **achievement** in improving your diet and health in the **long** term, just like an exercise plan. Woven into the book are the mind–body responses, case studies and comments from people who have applied this programme, to support you through this process. There are:

• No total exclusion of foods — just **timings** of when to eat them,

• No supplements or products, just wonderful **food**, and

• No 'X' number of day plan to follow but a **regular routine** to build into your lifestyle.

This **weekly** routine can help you rebalance your diet to enable you to:

• Discover your own body's **wisdom**,

• **Harmonise** with the daily, monthly and yearly patterns of your body, and

• Utilise the **power** of nature to reactivate the elimination phase.


## Comments from people who have experienced this programme:

**Karen after her second Rebalance:**

"Since starting the course I have noticed that my stomach no longer feels bloated or uncomfortable after eating meals."

**Patricia after four weeks of the Rebalance programme:**

"The eczema-type rashes on my hands have gone, my complexion looks brighter and I feel less bloated."

**Phil after three sessions of the Rebalance programme:**

"My energy levels are back up and I am sleeping a lot better. Even my partner noticed."

**Yvonne after three weeks on the programme:**

"When I first contacted Alison, I was really worried about the eating pattern I was in.

I was addicted to sugar and eating vast amounts of chocolate. I now drink two litres of water a day, my appetite has reduced, and I no longer crave a sugar fix. I am continuing to drink more water throughout the day and eating only when I feel hungry. Thank you for your help and I am glad this was something I tried."

**Annabel after four sessions over three months:**

"Alison has helped me after a year of stress and bereavement to be able to take control of my diet and lifestyle. She has helped with breathing exercises and learning to take time to adjust my daily life. I now feel much more energised and in control of my feelings, and my family have noticed I am nearly back to my normal self."

**Patricia after six months:**

"I have always wanted to do a detox, but it never felt right, but after meeting Alison I finally decided to have a go. I lost one stone gradually over six months and feel a lot better with more energy."

All these people have benefited from a simple food-based solution without drugs or supplements. So how does it work? This is what we discuss in the next chapter.

# Chapter 1

# Benefits of a Simple Food-Based Solution

*The doctors of the future will no longer treat the human frame with drugs but rather will cure and prevent disease with nutrition.*

*– unknown*

## Why Rebalance Your Diet?

Rebalancing your diet by eating less and drinking more water gives your body the chance to rest not just external activity, but internally too, something we do not do enough of in our lifestyle today. It allows the whole digestive tract to cleanse and rest, ready for *effective* absorption. It also helps clear out the unhelpful bacteria and promote the good.

During your rebalancing period you are eating alkaline-forming foods with low GI (Glycaemic Index), drinking water and establishing eating routines at particular times to get back into balance with your internal organs. To discover the best formula for you is what this course is all about! It is like starting exercise after a long break – you build it up slowly, step by step.

## Aims and Objectives

In this book I aim to help you find a new routine and relationship with food to assist you to rebalance on a daily, weekly and/or monthly basis. We will achieve this together by finding out about your body's natural rhythms and its unique tendencies which will be dynamic, changing with your internal and external environment. Over time you will become familiar with the internal 'weather' of your digestive system, helping you eat intuitively with your body's wisdom.

## Diets

Diets have a bad reputation as people do not seem to be able to stick to them! Some people go on a diet to lose weight but end up putting weight on!

Some diets are designed to bring something back into balance and are not intended to be followed all the time! Diets can bring about a yo-yo effect and in extreme cases can cause more harm than good. The Rebalance plan that I am suggesting is not a diet as such. It is a way of bringing back the yin and yang of eating, the rhythm of absorption and elimination. We have just got out of balance by absorbing all the time and not giving our bodies the chance to eliminate! Life is about oscillation. We have the day and night, the seasons, the Moon phases. We need to return to the oscillation of absorption and elimination. We often have problems absorbing because we have not allowed time for the elimination phase. This programme brings this balance back into play and can improve the absorption process.

## My Story

I have been following a rebalance routine for several years and now eat half the amount of food that I used to, have more energy and have lost weight. I put this down to eating lighter meals that are food combined (no carbohydrates with protein); this has improved my digestion, so I have more energy, which in turn gives me the inspiration to exercise more.  My rebalance routine helped me *see* where I could adjust my *daily* routines in a realistic step-by-step process. I have used this Rebalance programme to recover from various health issues (miscarriage, skin conditions) and to help me through the transitional period of the menopause. I now use it to strengthen my immune system and maintain a clear digestion. All through a simple food-based solution.

As I continue to work with more people, they too are looking for this simple food-based solution and for help through transitions in life.

So how do we use the Moon phases to rebalance our diet? This is what we will find out in the next chapter.

# Chapter 2

# The Power of Aligning Your Meals with the Moon and Your Body's Organs

*'The Power of Timing'*
*– Johanna Paungge and Thomas Poppe*

## Daily Rhythm of Our Organs

This is an exciting subject to get into when rebalancing your diet. It helps the process immensely. This is being used more and more in the realms of health as it is no longer mythical as we see it in the tides, menstrual patterns and in our circadian rhythms.  In Johanna Paungger and Thomas Poppe's book "The Power of Timing" they explain all kinds of activities to be aligned with the moon. Andreas Moritz's book "Timeless Secrets of Health and Rejuvenation" discusses the biological clock and how that can be utilised in your life. The schedule "Daily Rhythms of Your Organs" shown in Chapter 9 lists all the daily rhythms of our internal organs. The key points to make are:

The pancreas reaches its peak at 11am and then starts its low phase. Most people feel a drop in energy at this time. The heart then enters its peak phase. If we do some light exercise here, this can raise our blood sugar level *without* taking in food and increase the level of oxygen, helping brain function. Try to follow this as best you can when on your rebalance day.

The liver reaches its low phase at night, so making your evening meal light supports your liver to do its other job of cellular regeneration and takes the burden away of digesting food late at night.

The bladder reaches its peak time between 3 and 5pm, so drink plenty of **water** in the afternoon to support your bladder (and kidneys). This helps reduce the food cravings in the evening when we often think we are hungry when in fact we are thirsty.

Just doing these three things makes the difference between riding a wave and missing the wave when surfing! It may take a few practice runs before you get the hang of it. Sometimes when you are out of balance, changing habits can seem unsettling. You may feel like you are drinking when you do not want to, but this could be only because you are changing your routine. Stick with it. Eventually, the new routine will feel more in rhythm with your body.

## My Story

When I first started to apply this new routine of drinking in the afternoon, I felt a bit weird, but I realised the benefits in the evening when I did not feel hungry. After a few months of applying this new rebalancing routine for 24 hours every week I found that I wanted to do this daily, not just on my rebalance days. This is just one example of how having a weekly rebalance day shows you what your body really wants. It provides the contrast for you to understand more clearly.

## Monthly Rhythms of Our Bodies

The Moon dictates the peaks of eliminating and absorbing, for both women and men. When we are on a **full** Moon our bodies are at the peak of **absorption**. Taking in fluids is easiest on a full Moon. On a **new** Moon (no visible Moon in the sky) we are at our peak of **eliminating**. If we ride this wave then it all becomes easier, even for men!

During the **waning** Moon, that is when the Moon is travelling from full to new, there is a **detoxifying** effect on the body, and it reaches a peak at the **new** Moon.

On the **waxing** Moon, that is when the Moon is travelling from new to full, there is a building up and **absorption** effect on the body.

You may get different reactions to your rebalance day depending on the phase of the Moon and time of year. See how you respond to the different phases; it may help you understand a lot more if you are wondering why you are reacting differently (more energy, harder work, more hunger or no hunger etc).

So how do we start this process? This is what we will find out in the next chapter.

# Chapter 3

# The Importance of Starting with the Corners

## Building Your Own Inner Compass

## The Importance of Starting with the Corners

By starting with the corners of a jigsaw, we all know it makes it a lot easier to put the other pieces into place. And it is the same with our diet. Over time, I have found this the most effective way to see the wood from the trees so to speak. This develops into your inner compass on deciding what to eat. These four corners are:

1. Rehydrate Your Body

2. Alkaline and acid balance

3. Obtaining a stable blood sugar level

4. And finally, oxygen

We are motivated to eat due to hunger, and just like our tears where we have tears of joy, laughter, sadness and pain, we can have hunger for water, comfort, salt, warmth and oxygen as well as food. Our body can also stimulate the hunger reflex because we are out of balance with too much acid in our body. We can experience hunger if we have low blood sugar levels. If we get all these four aspects into balance (water, alkaline balance, stabilise blood sugar and keep oxygen levels up) we may not have the desire to eat and yet *still* feel satisfied. This is what we are aiming towards in our 24-Hour Rebalance so we can rest the digestive system and still feel no desire to eat. Once we come out of the Rebalance, we are far more in tune to choose what our body actually wants to eat, and we have a better alignment of our food choices.

So let us have a look at these four corners in more detail in the next chapter.

# Chapter 4

# The Jigsaw Method

## A Holistic System for Bringing Your Health

## Back into Balance

# First Corner of the Jigsaw: Rehydrate Your Body

This is the number one area to address if you are interested in rebalancing your diet. Yes, it is not just about food! Your body will not be able to rebalance your diet if you are dehydrated. This is because we often feel hungry when in fact our body really needs water. We often misread a feeling of hunger meaning 'I need food' when in fact our body is just thirsty. When you start to rebalance your diet regularly, on a weekly basis, you will begin to feel the difference between hunger and thirst.

## How Do I Know if I Am dehydrated?

Generally, adults need to drink about two to four litres of water a day, depending on environment, level of exercise, body size etc. If you are drinking very little, initially you will need to drink water even if you are not thirsty. Ideally, we want to be tuned into our body's thirst stimulus when we get dehydrated. So how do we get tuned in to this if we are currently dehydrated?

## If I Am Not Thirsty, Surely I Am Not Dehydrated?

We often ignore a message from our body. Stress, food, unflavoursome water and inconvenience can prevent us from satisfying this message of thirst our body is sending us. If we continue this pattern, our body **stops** sending this message and the drought goes deeper into our body, giving us other symptoms such as wakeful nights, indigestion, migraine and joint problems to name just a few.

## How Do I Get Back into Balance where I Feel Thirsty, and I Satisfy That Need?

It is best to increase your intake of water gradually until you are drinking at least two litres a day. This is a guide: your size, diet, environment and lifestyle may vary so you may need more. This excludes all other drinks including **naturally caffeine-free teas** as these *often* have a diuretic effect, satisfying our thirst stimulus but **not** rehydrating our bodies. Our bodies are most dehydrated in the morning, so you could start substituting/adding drinks in the morning to help support the process of rehydration. Once you have established a routine of about two litres a day, tune into your body's needs to accommodate your changing environment. You may notice it being clearer. Here is an example of how your body begins to communicate thirst again.

## My Story

I had been drinking two litres of water a day for several years and I live and work in the country. I then had to conduct some interviews in an air-conditioned office, with fluorescent lighting and no windows! I noticed that I had to drink an extra three mugs of water that day as I felt dehydrated and had a headache coming on. Years ago, I used to work in an office every day and drank just half a mug of water in the morning. I had no sense of thirst but suffered headaches regularly. Now when I do get the odd headache, I always try drinking water first.

When you have your rebalance day you will be drinking more water than usual, giving you the contrast in order to be able to notice your own body's needs. Over time you will be able to not only distinguish thirst from hunger more easily but also realise the quantity of water you really need.

## Caffeine

We all know caffeine causes dehydration. It will satisfy our thirst but actually takes water from your body. Very counter productive! So, if you are an excessive caffeine drinker aim to reduce your caffeine drinks and substitute **one** caffeine drink with a cup of hot water. Even caffeine-*free* drinks do not rehydrate you as water does, as they are often diuretic. Keep substituting one a day every two or three days until you are down to just one or occasionally two per day or, if you want to, none per day.

Once your body has adjusted, a caffeine drink will feel like a massive injection of stimulant! And now you will be able to see the contrast! You could start by substituting caffeine drinks that you have towards the end of the day to promote better sleep. If it all sounds too severe, just try it on your rebalance day first, or whichever first step suits you.

## Why Do We Rehydrate Gradually?

Full rehydration can take up to a year. We are like a dried-up pot of soil. If you pour lots of water on the dried pot it all just comes out of the other end. A bit of water at a time for dried pots is much better. The same applies to us. Why is this? When the body is short of water it builds up a layer of cholesterol round the cell to prevent further loss of water. This reduces cell membrane permeability, in other words things can't get **into** the cell so easily, including water. When we drink more water, the body then needs to remove the cholesterol layer **before** the water can enter the cell. So, rehydration is a process that needs repeating over a period of time.

Stress also causes the body to build up cholesterol around the cell lining. This is the physiological effect of stress. Our bodies perceive the stress as threatening and undergo a preservation reaction. This causes the body to lay down cholesterol to preserve the cells from any threats. So, finding ways of actively reducing stress or eliminating it is an essential practice in your rebalance routine.

## Caffeine, Stress and Cholesterol

Too much caffeine causes the body to go into a stress reaction and can cause the body to lay down cholesterol. Cholesterol is a fat and people can be misled into thinking that if their cholesterol levels are too high, they need to reduce fat in their diet. This can be a mistake if you are dehydrated and/or stressed. What you really need is to increase water and reduce, or find ways of eliminating, some of your stress.

## My Story – Mary, IT Supervisor

Before I started my first Rebalance course, I drank no water and had about three cups of caffeinated drinks a day. I consider myself to have been slightly stressed at work and had a slightly high cholesterol level which had been creeping up over the years. I began swapping one mug of coffee a day for one cup of water. After a few days I noticed I was thirsty after eating an oat cake. Incidentally, I was due a cholesterol check after my second week on the Rebalance programme and it had gone down by two points. I can only put it down to this programme as nothing else had changed.

If you are sceptical of the cholesterol levels being reduced after such a short period of time, consider the fact that rehydration improves *all* cellular functioning as it improves membrane permeability and encourages transportation of essential nutrients and hormonal messages.

## Avoiding and Eliminating Stress

I use these two terms: 'avoiding' and 'eliminating'. Some stress can be avoided, for example I do not go to a disco on a Friday night, or drive the car at some illegal speed, or organise a big family Christmas gathering! These are stressful to me, and I can avoid them! You may be able to look at your lifestyle and decide "Yes I can avoid that one!"

Some stresses are not avoidable, but you can eliminate the effects of the stress. On a daily basis, I practice yoga and meditation and get into the zone of deep relaxation. To some people this may mean taking the dog for a walk and having a meditative time. Have a go at building some deep relaxation into your rebalance routine and then build it into your **daily** routine. This is a huge investment in your health. The Alexander Technique is a method to help you with this process and there are teachers all over the world. The UK web site is: www.alexandertechnique.co.uk.

The practice of "Throat Smile" is a practical, accessible routine that you can use and is described in Chapter 9. You could also try going to a class and learning some methods to help you on this road. There are many audio products on the market to guide you through deep relaxation. Ask a friend if they could recommend any.

## Insulin and Cholesterol

It is believed that high levels of insulin in the blood, over long periods of time, can cause cholesterol to be laid down. Coronary artery disease is caused by plaque building up in the walls of the arteries that supply blood to the heart, called coronary arteries. Plaque is made up of cholesterol deposits. Plaque build-up causes the inside of the arteries to narrow over time. This process is called **atherosclerosis**. So, a high carbohydrate diet (which causes insulin to rise), plus stress, plus dehydration is to be avoided. See the Balancing Your GIs section for more information in Chapter 4.

# Second Corner of the Jigsaw: Alkaline–Acid Balance

## What Is this Alkaline pH All About?

The term pH is a measurement of the amount of acid or alkaline in liquids or solids. A pH of one is the most acid and, a pH of 14 is the most alkaline, with seven being neutral. Some obvious acidic foods include rhubarb, but meat and fish produce an acid effect once we have **absorbed** them. Alkaline foods are less easily noticeable, but they include most vegetables. The pH levels in your body act a bit like the temperature. We all know that if it is too cold, we do not function so well; our muscles tighten, our joints start to ache and in extreme cases, our circulation ceases. If we are too hot, we feel lethargic and don't seem to be able to get enough air; in extreme cases we can burn. This happens on a cellular level, and we can feel it.

Now just like temperature, pH balance affects our cellular activity, but we just don't feel it so well. So, when we are too hot, cold things feel great! When we are too cold, hot things feel great (or at least warm things!). When we are too acid, alkaline foods don't always feel great! The pH balancing mechanism for foods has really got screwed up as our food is too rich and overstimulating for our tastebuds. We must follow some guidelines to get us back in balance. This is how your rebalance day can really help you.

## OK, So How Do I Find Out My Body's pH Value?

So how do we know what our pH value is? Unfortunately, it is not that easy as we have various liquids in our bodies that have varying pH values. For example, our stomach naturally has a low pH (that is acid) to digest food and kill off bacteria. Our pH in our colon is higher (more alkaline) than in our small intestine. The muscles, brain cells and blood cells really like a slightly alkaline value, but we can't measure this very easily. We can use a pH tester that we may be able to obtain from the doctor or from the internet, but this only measures the fluid it is put in. But why not try rebalancing your body's **intuition** so that you just know when you are too acid? We can start this process by looking at the total content of our food and say, to get a pH value of 7.5 (the ideal balance) just over 50% of what we eat needs to be alkaline-forming foods.

However, we also get our body's pH from the air that we breathe, the water that we drink and our environment. So, to maintain our optimum pH we need to look at all these things too. Unfortunately, the air that we breathe, the water that we drink, and our environment is very acid due to air pollution, pesticides and radiation from wi-fi, mobile phones, computers, cars, TVs etc. So, the alkaline/acid food balance needs to be more like 70–80% alkaline in the western world. Also, if we are already too acid then we need to maybe eat 90% alkaline for a time until we get more into balance. On your Rebalance you need to aim to eat 95–100% alkaline-forming foods. You then start to *cherry pick* which foods you like and start to introduce these into the rest of your week's diet, so you are **aiming** for about 70–80% alkaline-forming foods depending on your lifestyle.

## So Which Foods Are Alkaline Forming?

The foods that we eat can sometimes take on a different property once they have been absorbed. Lemons are a great example. They are clearly acid but once they are absorbed, they are the most alkaline-forming food you can eat with a pH value of 14. This is why we use the term 'alkaline-forming foods'. The foods transform into alkaline once they are absorbed. Here is a summary of alkaline/acid forming foods:

**Alkaline-forming foods:** All fruit and vegetables with a few exceptions such as: blueberries, canned or glazed fruits, cranberries, currants, plums, prunes, olives and cooked tomatoes. There are a few nuts and seeds that are also alkaline forming; these are almonds, pumpkin seeds and millet.

**Acid-forming foods:** *All* grains and pulses are acid forming. These include bread, pasta, beans, rice and flour. *All* animal, fish and poultry protein are acid forming. All nuts and seeds are acid forming with the above exceptions of almonds, pumpkin seeds and millet. A few fruits and vegetables are also acid forming, and these are blueberries, canned or glazed fruits, cranberries, currants, plums, prunes, olives and cooked tomatoes.

**Neutral-forming foods:** Quinoa, eggs, butter, yoghurt, cream, raw cows milk and vegetable oils.

So, most proteins and carbohydrates are acid forming. In fact, you may be realising that most of your diet is carbohydrate or animal protein which, *once absorbed*, forms an acid pH in your body.

This is a general guide: the pH value may vary depending on whether the food is organic or non-organic, or whether you eat the whole food or part of the food. For example, egg yolk is slightly acid forming whereas egg white is slightly alkaline forming. The key is *on your rebalance day you want to aim for 99% alkaline forming*, the rest of the week you are *moving towards* 70–80% alkaline-forming foods, due to our lifestyle, which causes a lot of build-up of acid within our body. *Moving towards* is very important – see below.

## Take it Easy – One Step At a Time

You may be feeling a bit worried, but the good news is it's always best to take one step at a time. Your body needs to adjust to this new diet. You may substitute one meal a day and make it totally alkaline forming. Or you may just start by having a freshly squeezed lemon diluted in water every morning and change nothing else in your diet. Gradually you may begin to notice a difference. Particularly if you divert from this new routine and see how you feel. Your body really only reports changes, so notice how you feel when you have changed something.

## My Story – Jane, IT Support

Years ago, I used to have stomach cramps after eating an apple in the morning. At the time I did not eat any fruit or vegetables apart from peas and sweetcorn! Over the years I gradually started to avoid gluten and eat more quinoa and millet as my main carbohydrate. I ate more vegetables substituting a bowl of steamed vegetables for my evening meal once or twice a week. I also generally started to eat more vegetables with my other main meals including carrots, broccoli and potatoes. Now I can eat an apple for breakfast with no stomach cramps.

## Why Did Jane Get Stomach Cramps After Eating an Apple Which Is Alkaline Forming?

In some cases, the pH in our stomach (which is naturally very acidic) is too acidic! This could be caused by long term stress and/or eating too many acid-forming foods. When an apple is eaten and arrives in the stomach, because it is slightly acidic (but remember, once absorbed is alkaline forming) it can tip the scales too far. Eating an apple first thing in the morning can then create the scenario of the 'straw that broke the camel's back'. Once Jane had got her body's general pH level back into balance, her stomach's pH adjusted so she was able to eat an apple first thing in the morning with no repercussions.

## Two Important Points to Make

When you start your journey to rebalance your pH it may be advisable to introduce more vegetables in your diet and wait a few weeks/months before introducing fruit. This then may avoid the above scenario.

Antacids **decrease** your stomach's acid level but still do not address the problem of the rest of your body's pH value; in fact, they can also interfere with the rest of your body's digestion process and cause more problems down the line!

## My Story – Rachel, Therapist

I had been eating well for a few years and felt I was back into balance with my pH levels. However, occasionally I would have a binge on acid-forming carbohydrates – homemade chocolate biscuits made with spelt flour and maple syrup – how could I resist them! I thought I was going to be OK as they had no sugar in and no wheat. I noticed I was short tempered, irritable and low spirited. This started only a few hours after eating these biscuits. Once I realised, I focused on eating 90% alkaline for that day. I already started to feel better after the first meal. The next day I felt back to normal, good natured and high-spirited.

## Summary

Alkaline forming foods have a **high** pH value and are generally the ones we need **more** of to rebalance our bodies' cellular pH level. These are generally vegetables, most fruits and pumpkin seeds, millet and almonds.

Acid-forming foods have a **low** pH value and are the ones we generally need to eat **less** of to rebalance our cellular pH level. These are all meat, all pulses, all grains, most seeds and nuts, and include bread, pasta, oats, most cheeses, fish, chicken meat and soya.

Please note that we are very used to the term *low* – low calories, low sugar, low GI. Everything is advised to be low but with the alkaline/acid balance we want a high pH value (that is, alkaline forming).

# Third Corner of The Jigsaw: Balancing Your GIs

Your Glycaemic Index (GI) measures how fast the sugar (including carbohydrates) enters your blood causing your blood sugar levels to rise. Eating lower GI foods helps balance your body's blood sugar levels, which in turn can help balance mood swings, food cravings and increase the power of your immune system. Reducing sugars and carbohydrates also helps balance your microflora, that is your gut flora, the basis of all absorption. All these positive benefits of eating foods with a lower GI really give you that incentive to practice a regular rebalance day. This is because it is most important to eat foods with a low GI, on your rebalance day. Some fruit and vegetables that appear 'healthy', and wholefood, still have a high GI, for example, pineapple, potatoes and parsnips, and so are still best to be avoided on your **rebalance day**.

## Increasing Our Foods With a Low GI

This is a key issue in our western diets that **often** have *too many* carbohydrates. A table of GI foods can be found on the internet. But the timing of eating is also key. Low GI foods are best eaten in the morning and higher GI foods towards the second half of the day. Generally **complex** carbohydrates (e.g., bread, pasta and rice) have a *moderate* GI, simple carbohydrates (e.g., fruit juice, raw cane sugar, bananas, dates) have a *high* GI, and protein and most vegetables (except potatoes) have a *low* GI.

Rather than looking up charts, you may find it easier to look at the *taste* of the foods – so, if it tastes sweet it is high GI, if it is slightly sweet, e.g., bread or pasta, it is medium GI, and if it tastes bitter, pungent or sour then they are generally low GI. This is why very ripe, sweet tasting fruit will have a different effect to underripe, less sweet-tasting fruit. Using the 'taste dial' is a useful guide. When you are on your *rebalance day* you are already avoiding **complex** carbohydrates as these are acid forming. However, we cannot talk about balancing GIs without talking about microflora first.

## Microflora

In the long term it is the microflora we are trying to balance (reducing the unhelpful bacteria and increasing the good). On our rebalance day we are not feeding the unhelpful bacteria and so they die within our gut and cellular system. If we have an overabundance of the unhelpful bacteria, then we may be advised to follow a diet that has no carbohydrate for a few months. I feel this is too extreme and suggest this Rebalance programme may be more achievable with less of a shock to your system. It also helps you to establish new **routines** that you can apply long term which may address the **initial cause** of the problem.

## Quick Fix Versus Long-Term Gain

Rebalancing your microflora is a process that takes time. It is like building up good quality organic soil in your garden. It may take several years if it is very depleted. Enjoy the process of feeling better each day rather than thinking of a quick fix. If you currently eat carbohydrates for breakfast, consider moving this to your evening meal (or at least lunchtime) and gradually substitute with a protein-based breakfast with non-starchy vegetables, your rebalance day will help you on the road towards this transition. You may also notice an increase in energy as you start to eat in tune with your body, which digests carbohydrates more easily in the afternoon and early evening.

## Understanding Microflora and Sweet Cravings

It is useful to know about microflora from the start when you are trying to balance your GIs as we often have cravings for something sweet; it is **not** our bodies that crave it, it is the bacteria within us. For every human cell we have 10 bacterial cells! We are therefore more bacteria than our cellular selves! So, when we have these cravings, we can remind ourselves that it is not always us but the bacteria within us that cause the cravings.

This is why we often are in two minds over what we want to eat. Another good book on this subject is 'The Body Ecology Diet' by Donna Gates. She talks about the big die-off phase where the bacteria start to die off and your body is clearing out the dead cells. You may feel a detox reaction where you feel weak and run down as your body has the overhead of clearing things out. So, getting rehydrated is again the number one step on your Rebalance programme to make this process easier.

Can I still have a microflora imbalance if I do not eat lots of carbohydrates?

If you do not have a high carbohydrate diet, you could still have a bacteria imbalance due to antibiotics. Antibiotics kill off bacteria but unfortunately do not kill fungi. This causes your microbiome to get out of balance and can increase the fungal levels which could contribute to a candida overgrowth. So, after a course of antibiotics, you need to reintroduce the good bacteria which aim to return your microbiome back into balance including the fungi candida. Candida is a helpful fungus for digestion in *small* quantities. It is unhelpful in large quantities as it starts to dissolve away the gut lining. This is the benefit of your Rebalance programme when for a period of 24 hours you can consume minimum carbohydrates and rebalance your microbiome on a regular basis.

## January

In January we often are recovering from the overindulgence of Christmas and using the Rebalance programme at this time of year brings this aspect of balancing GIs into full bloom. Low GI foods over 24 hours once a week can really help you get back into balance. You can then start to cherry pick aspects of the rebalance period which you enjoy and add them into your **daily** diet for the remainder of the week and start to feel the benefits.

## Sweeteners

Please note, sweeteners are not advisable as this gives you the experience that you are about to eat a high GI food, so your body starts to produce insulin to maintain blood sugar levels, but as no sugar enters your bloodstream you effectively get a *drop* in blood sugar levels which causes the hunger reflex to be ignited. So, I suggest avoiding sweet-tasting foods that have no sugar in them; this also includes stevia and liquorice tea.

# Fourth Corner of The Jigsaw: Oxygen

Yes, we can experience a raise in energy levels from oxygen. Sometimes when we experience hunger, it is our body trying to tell us we need oxygen and not food. This is why, when you are on your rebalance, if you get hungry between meals then I suggest light exercise. Headaches may also be alleviated with light exercise. Once you get to experience this, you can see it more clearly and start to anticipate it too.

There are some muscles that can utilise more energy from oxygen than others and some believe that the postural muscles can obtain energy solely from oxygen. So, our 'hunger' could be not for food but oxygen. This programme helps you experience this in practice, raising energy levels and satisfying hunger through *light* exercise. The key is *light* exercise as the muscles that can obtain more energy from oxygen contract slowly. So, wherever you are in your fitness capabilities, remember *light* exercise is key.

On the programme you can use this aspect when you are working towards avoiding eating between meals. After you have applied this programme for several months you may want to experience a breatharian meal where you are purely consuming oxygen and sunlight to satisfy your 'hunger' at a given mealtime on your rebalance. Knowledge of your body's biorhythms helps remind you that you will go through a phase and then it can pass.

I would like to add this is not the place to discuss the possibility of a total breatharian 'diet'. I do feel that we are here on the planet to experience the joy of eating. This process is purely for you to help rebalance your digestion in order for you to **enjoy** your food more for the rest of the week.

So how does all this work in practice? The next chapter goes though the 24-hour guide. There is a different process for each season so wherever you are, read the season you are in now. Remember to read the section on General Points For All Seasons when making the recipes. So, is your current season autumn, winter, summer or spring? Move on to your relevant season and read on.

# Chapter 5

# Autumn

*'Body Ecology' – Donna Gates*

# The Autumn Rebalance Programme

Autumn is the most challenging transitional season as we adjust to the colder climate and our bodies must turn to the contraction phase of autumn after the expansive phase of the summer season. For us to do this we need to start to slow down the activities of life and prepare for the hibernation period of winter. Nature starts to lose its leaves and retreat underground. If we ride this wave, it gives us an opportunity to address the cleansing of our bowels to create a clear digestive lining. This gives our good bacteria the advantage over the unhelpful bacteria, creating a healthy microbiome. This is the foundation of a strong immune system and reduced bloating in our abdomen.

## The Autumn Bugs

During the winter we often start to get bugs and infections. One theory behind this is that these bugs enter our bodies through the *lining* of our digestive tract *first*, and then travel through the body, eventually finding their way to various parts such as the throat. It is hard to believe this until you begin to experience it. Stress weakens the body, causing the bacteria to get out of balance. This eventually makes the gut lining too permeable thus allowing the bugs to enter which then find themselves in various locations in our body. A clear digestive tract with a healthy lining can help keep the bugs to a minimum reducing the burden on our immune system; plus, the good bacteria reduce stress in our body which also supports our immune system. Eating foods that **cleanse** the gut and **rebuild** a healthy lining help us prepare a good foundation for winter.

## Time of Resting

We naturally have the instinct to retreat to our homes as the nights draw in. Respect this process when you are doing your rebalance day and go gently with yourself, allowing yourself to rest more and so reducing the level of stress is key. The '**Active Resting Position**' described in Chapter 9 is a great practice to help eliminate stress. This is a good practice for other times too! Remember your body notices **contrasts** not *constants*. As autumn is the hardest season to adjust to, the daily demands of life may feel too challenging, so allow yourself to make your rebalance day simple or just do a shadow until things calm down a little. Here is an example of a shadow.

## Mary's Story — Single Working Mum Going through the Menopause

I had been doing a regular rebalance for a few years and then my menopause started. As autumn approached, I realised that my rebalance day was very challenging with my children at new schools and starting a divorce, so I had a lot going on in my personal life. I decided to just allow myself a bowl of soup and/or stewed fruit for the evening. Then in the morning I could have my normal breakfast. Because I had maintained this over the autumn, I was able to go back to my usual Rebalance programme over the winter. If I had not done this in the autumn, I think I would have found it too challenging to rebalance during the winter months and would have totally lost this routine. This not only helped me to keep my weight in balance but also kept my immune system strong, so I was not prone to so many infections.

If you apply this 24-hour rebalance period *regularly* in the autumn, this can lay the foundation for your immune system to be able to ward off infections during the winter. But remember to go gently if it is your first rebalancing as stress can counteract the benefit of the food, so learn from Mary's story.

## Foods for Autumn

Focusing on foods that cleanse and promote elimination supports the autumn process. These include celery and plums as they have an **astringent** property on our body and can help 'squeeze out' the toxins. On your rebalance day we also need to ensure we keep **warm even though we are eating less**, so all the food for our rebalance period gives us **warming properties** such as, kale, ginger and fennel. Nurturing soups that help us adjust to the change in climate are excellent at this time, so use them to supplement a meal, replace a meal or even as a snack using a lighter soup.

Autumn is a key time to ensure that your microbiome is well supported which in turn helps support your immune system. **Sauerkraut** is a natural probiotic and an excellent salad to eat in the colder months as it has a warming influence on your body. If you are new to sauerkraut, introducing it at this time gives you a really good start to rebalancing your microbiome, however, go steady with the quantity initially; see Chapter 9 on 'New to Sauerkraut'. You do not want to overdo it as you may be put off and lose the benefit, a bit like doing exercise: too much too soon is unpleasant, but gentle progress can improve your health.

If you already eat sauerkraut, then you can also use it as a snack between meals as it is an excellent cleanser for your gut and eating it on a relatively empty stomach supports this process even more. You may be surprised how it can satisfy your hunger between meals.

**Linseeds** are an excellent food to ensure regular bowel movements. These are soaked to ensure easier digestion and absorption. They are in your final meal on your rebalance day to ensure your bowels keep moving after your period of reduced intake of food. On your normal days you could eat them two or three times a day too. Just one teaspoon soaked for eight hours.

**Pears** also have an elimination effect on our body and are in abundance at this time of year.

**Pumpkins** are also in plentiful supply during autumn, and these make a very nurturing and heart-warming drink when you simmer with the skins, stalks and leaves of other vegetables (see potassium broth recipe). Include the seeds of the pumpkin to utilise the whole vegetable.

## British Winter Time

In Britain in autumn our clocks move backwards by one hour to winter time, which causes all our rhythms to get out of balance. If you can aim towards the British **summer** times (during the winter months) with the internal rhythms of your organs (see Chapter 9 '**Daily Rhythms of Your Organs**') this will help you eat in sync with your body during the winter. This may be hard to do on your *normal* days but at least you can get back into balance on your rebalance day. Your rebalance day may help with just *reducing* the quantity of food you eat in the evening for the remainder of the week. This will not only keep your weight in balance and help on food costs, but also promotes better digestion and so maintains your balanced microbiome.

## Key Points to Take Away

1. Autumn is the time of year of greatest adjustment.

2. Autumn is a great wave to ride for cleansing your digestive lining.

3. Helpful foods at this time of year include those that have: **astringent** properties (celery, plums), **elimination** properties (linseeds, pears), **warming properties** (kale, fennel, ginger, pumpkins) and **probiotics** (sauerkraut).

4. Work towards smaller meals in the evening that are warming and nurturing still. If you do not wish to lose weight, then make your midday meal larger rather than your evening meal.

5. Clean and healthy gut lining encourages resistance to the winter bugs.

# The 24-Hour Autumn Guide

**Your 24-Hour Weekly Programme – Contents, What to Do with Them and When to Eat Them!**

Start your Rebalance programme at your *evening meal.* If you normally have a mid-afternoon snack, then have that still. Soak your pumpkin seeds in water overnight in the *fridge.* Bold items are your drinks/food.

## Evening Meal

**Evening Soup** – heat and enjoy ideally by 6pm, no later than 7pm.

Drink one mug of warm water if you are still hungry after your evening meal. Stop drinking and eating after 8pm.

**Breakfast –** brush tongue and teeth before drinking or eating, then drink one mug of warm water. Remove pumpkin seeds from fridge and drain off the water, leave covered for later.

**Stewed pear and ginger** (or stewed plums and ginger)

Then sip one mug of warm water.

After 30 minutes *if you are hungry* have the morning **soup.**

**Mid-morning snack –** if you have a headache, then drink water, try to do some light exercise and/or rest.  See Chapter 9 for 'My Rescue Plan *if* I Get Hungry or Have a Headache'. Check that you are not on the turning point of your pancreas going into the low phase (see The Daily Rhythms of Your Internal Organs – Chapter 9); you may just need to rest whilst your body changes gear and it will pass. Your mind will trick you into thinking this is only going to get worse but stay with the process of trying all three (drinking, resting and light exercise), as in most cases it passes. Again, if you are still hungry before lunch then drink another mug of warm water. You can drink as many as three mugs of water if you like. If you are still hungry *and feel you need to eat* something do not push yourself as this stresses your body; have your **soaked pumpkin seeds**. However, you may be able to last out until lunchtime before eating.

**Lunchtime –** if you are hungry have the **alkaline yog sub,** this may satisfy you until mid-afternoon or evening but if you are still hungry *have your lunch*. This is a key time for you to connect to your body's wisdom, ask yourself 'what do I feel like eating?' Our digestive enzymes are at their *most active* at lunch time so eat well and try to keep your evening meal light. You may find you are satisfied with a much smaller amount at lunch time **and** in the evening - this is your body rebalancing the volume of food. Or you may find you have a smaller lunch and a snack in the afternoon and then a lighter evening meal. Ensure you stop drinking and eating after

8pm so your body maintains the rhythm of eating a lighter meal in the evening. The next day you may find you are surprisingly less hungry than usual with renewed energy.

Enjoy your rebalance day.

# Chapter 6

# Winter

*How to Obtain Your Comfort and Nurturing with a Low Carbohydrate Diet*

# The Winter Rebalance Programme

Winter is the season where you have made the complete transition into the colder climate. We are now working with the real dormant phase in the seasons and need to slow down with the activities of life. However, this does not seem to happen with our lifestyle today as we start the run up to Christmas when we have another task on our hands along with the other things in our already hectic daily life. People often abandon looking after their diet and let go to indulge in the Christmas treats. By January, Christmas has passed, and we have a need to adjust to a healthier diet again.

This gives us an opportunity to address the amount of carbohydrates in our diet and so I emphasise this for the winter season. Balancing your glycaemic levels is one of the key aspects to help you rebalance your diet. This is because when we eat very low GI (Glycaemic Index) foods then we do not get the ups and downs of high and low sugar levels in our blood and so have reduced levels of 'hunger'. Once we realise this then it is a lot easier to eat just the right amount, rather than overeating. After this course people often report that they can eat much smaller amounts and are *still satisfied.*  Eating low GI foods also contributes towards balancing your microbiome which is at the heart of digestion and a strong immune system. See 'Third Pillar Balancing Your GIs'.

Once we get established at eating very low GI foods and our microbiome is more balanced, we realise nutrition is turned on its head as we get a lot of nutrients from bacteria in our gut. Michael Mosely has talked about this in his book "The Clever Guts Diet" and discusses how bacteria can actually affect your mood and behaviour too. Now back to how we can change our diet to build these helpful bacteria.

The food for your rebalance period gives you very low GI foods so when you go back to eating your 'normal' food you see how it affects your blood sugar levels. Remember, creating a contrast helps you notice things as your body will only report changes. This is why it is key to ask yourself 'What do I feel like after I have eaten this?' Your body is much more aware after your rebalance period so be poised to listen to your body when you go back to eating your 'usual' food. These feelings then give you information on what you actively want to choose to eat next time you complete your weekly rebalance.

## Susan's Story

After my Rebalance period, I grabbed a banana and shot out of the door to visit my Mum as she was poorly. I then got really hungry and as I was not at home, ended up snacking on a biscuit. By the time I finally got home in the evening I fell out with my son over something petty and ended up overeating at my evening meal as I was feeling sorry for myself.

This is an example of how a high GI food (banana) takes you to the ups and downs of low blood sugar. The banana raised Susan's blood sugar levels but then once her body had used up the banana her blood sugar levels plummeted causing her to feel hungry and then be too easily drawn to a biscuit, which was the only thing she felt was available to her (low blood sugar levels create an unhelpful environment causing us to make unclear decisions).

## The Winter Rebalance Programme

If we *create an environment* whereby we are in a *better place* to make *clearer* decisions for the benefit of our health, we are making progress! Planning your food and meals is key. This is why the guide for your Rebalance day is so important. This course is more about lifestyle nutrition.  People often talk about getting their head round the process. As you create a better environment for you and your microbiome, *you are in a better place* to get your head round the process involved. You may find that you can eat some carbohydrates in the evening, and it does not affect your blood sugar levels as much. So, if you feel a need for starchy or sweet food you can still eat your carbohydrates in the evening. This helps you to see how a low GI breakfast can actually sustain you for longer than a carbohydrate breakfast. After eating a very low GI breakfast, if you do get hungry in the morning, before lunch try drinking water – you may be thirsty rather than hungry – or do some exercise to raise your blood sugar levels. See 'My Rescue Plan if I Get Hungry or Have a Headache' in Chapter 9.  Over time you can adjust your usual breakfast to have lower and lower GI foods. People who often have porridge or oats for breakfast, thinking they are having a good start to the day, often report feeling heavy and lethargic afterwards. They then prefer the lower GI breakfast of protein (nuts or seeds for a lighter option) and vegetables (soup or steamed vegetables).

A great steppingstone from oat porridge to a lower GI breakfast is quinoa porridge. Use half and half to gradually get your body used to it.

## Before Christmas

If you are doing this programme before Christmas, you are laying a good environment for yourself not to be as drawn to the sweet foods over Christmas. You will also be building up a strong immune system to fight off the winter bugs. It will also be an easier ride for you when you are doing your weekly rebalance after Christmas.

## The Other Side of Christmas

If you are doing this programme on the other side of Christmas, you may have a detox reaction as your body eliminates the toxins and the dying off of the unhelpful bacteria which only survive in a sugar environment. Eating sauerkraut on your Rebalance programme may be of benefit to you as well. See Chapter 9 on 'New to Sauerkraut'.

# The 24-Hour Winter Guide

**Your 24-Hour Weekly Programme – Contents, What to Do with Them and When to Eat Them!**

Start your Rebalance programme at your evening meal. If you normally have a mid-afternoon snack, then still have that. Bold items are your drinks/food.

## Evening Meal

Evening Soup – heat and enjoy ideally by 6pm. No later than 7pm.

Drink 1 mug of warm water if you are still hungry after your evening meal. Stop drinking and eating after 8pm.

**Breakfast –** brush tongue and teeth before drinking or eating, then drink 1 mug of warm water.

**Grapefruit and ginger juice or equivalent drink**

Then sip 1 mug of warm water.

After 30 minutes if you are hungry have the **morning soup**.

**Mid-morning snack –** if you have a headache then drink water, try to do some light exercise and/or rest.  See Chapter 9 for 'My Rescue Plan *if* I Get Hungry or Have a Headache'. Check that you are not on the turning point of your pancreas going into the low phase (see The Daily Rhythms of Your Internal Organs – Chapter 9); you may just need to rest whilst your body changes gear and it will pass. Your mind will trick you into thinking this is only going to get worse, but stay with the process of trying all three (drinking, resting and light exercise), as in most cases it passes. Again, if you are still hungry before lunch then drink your mug of **potassium broth**. You can drink as many as three mugs of water if you like. If you are still hungry *and feel you need to eat* something do not push yourself as this stresses your body: have the **protein fix**. However, you may be able to last out until lunchtime before eating.

The **protein fix** may even substitute your lunch but if you are still hungry have your lunch. This is a key time for you to connect to your body's wisdom, ask yourself 'What do I feel like eating?' Our digestive enzymes are at their greatest activity at lunchtime so eat well and try to keep your evening meal light. You may find you are satisfied with a much smaller amount at lunchtime and in the evening: this is your body rebalancing the volume of food. Or you may find you have a smaller lunch and a snack in the afternoon and then a lighter evening meal. Ensure you stop drinking and eating after 8pm so your body maintains the rhythm of eating lighter meals in the evening. The next day you *may* find you are surprisingly less hungry than usual. Enjoy your rebalance day!

# Chapter 7

# Spring

*'Cellular Awakening' – Barbara Wren*

# The Spring Rebalance Programme

Spring is when there is a rising after the withdrawal of winter. Sap starts to rise up, trees, shoots start to appear from underground and nature is emerging from the earth. This also happens within us on a cellular level. As our body starts mobilising from deep within us this brings with it an *opportunity* for our body to eliminate deeply stored toxins. Use this wave of energy to your advantage and start a regular rebalance routine for the spring months. It is best to start simply, a routine that you can easily maintain.  Remember your body responds best to a regular pattern rather than a one-off, short-term fix. You can approach it with micro steps to avoid feeling overwhelmed.  This helps gain confidence, and gradual progress is always the best way. This will vary depending on your current lifestyle and health. It could mean a tongue brush first thing in the morning then a glass of warm water instead of a coffee. Or it could mean substituting your evening meal with a thin soup. And you can start with just once a week.

## The Spring Programme

Using the Rebalancing Your Diet programme for the spring months I emphasise eating alkaline-forming foods that also have properties which support the detox phase and ignite the detox reflex.  Having a curry soup in the evening helps your body start the process of detoxing. Adding cooking apples into your soup helps draw toxins out of your liver. A citrus fruit oil drink in the morning helps draw out toxins from the digestive tract. The property of lemon has a negative charge, so it attracts debris from your gut lining. Grapefruit juice helps draw out toxins from your joints (or use apples as a substitute if you have intolerance to grapefruit juice). Olive oil helps draw out toxins from your liver. It does this by purging the liver to produce bile which is the vehicle whereby your body can eliminate oil soluble toxins. Adding the option of garlic also helps this process. Cayenne pepper and ginger are also added to the drink to ensure your body stays warm, an essential component for your body to detox.

A nettle tea after the citrus drink provides your body with the essential minerals to continue the cellular process of detoxing without the burden of having to digest food. Drinking plenty of water keeps you hydrated for the toxins to be eliminated more easily. Resting helps your body have the energy and resources to continue the elimination process. A light soup may be all that you need for lunch as you discover new levels of energy and a loss of hunger after eliminating the toxins and hydrating your body. If you are hungry, though, have your lunch as this is the time your body is ripe for food from the digestive point of view. If you can make this as alkaline forming as possible this will support your body through the tail end of the rebalance period.

Applying this process regularly, once a week over the spring months, builds up your strength to detox your body. After a few weeks your body will start to anticipate this period making your rebalance easier.

## Taking It a Step Further with Your Spring Programme

Once you have completed a few weeks of the initial spring programme and you feel ready to take it a step further then you could increase the quantity of oil, garlic and ginger in the citrus oil drink. You may start with increasing it to two tablespoons of oil and twice as much garlic and ginger. Monitor how your body responds and if you feel it's right, increase it to four tablespoons of oil and four garlic cloves. You can also make your evening soup with more spices and garlic. Your body may have difficulties digesting the garlic so monitor your reaction. You may just want to increase the oil.

Or you may prefer to just repeat the process for 48 hours instead of 24 hours. What is more important is that you maintain the *regular* routine throughout spring. This helps your body get into a rhythm which means it can then start to *anticipate* the detox programme and utilise it more effectively. You are also able to cherry pick new ways of eating that you can build into the rest of the week. Once spring is over and the summer emerges you can then start your summer programme.

## Moon Phases

The waning Moon will make your detox easier and more powerful. You may feel on some weeks that you get a bigger reaction; for example, you may feel a surge of energy or a headache or increased tiredness. In extreme cases you can feel as if you are getting a cold. This is why I emphasise taking it step by step. Maybe try the first level for a whole month before increasing the quantity. Also allow yourself two steps forwards and one step backwards to ensure **long-term** progress. Once you get the hang of things you can increase the quantity on a new Moon, which is the peak phase of your body to detox, and then return to your normal quantity on the other weeks.

If you do end up getting a cold, remind yourself that illness sometimes is not just about fighting off an infection, it can also be a vehicle for your body to release emotional stress, so treat it as an opportunity to really rest and recuperate your energy.

## Nettles

These are amazing leaves and are in abundance in spring when they are sweet and soft. If you can pick your own this also gives you the lifestyle nutrition of fresh air, exercise and sunlight. They are naturally slug, rabbit and deer repellent and are easy to cultivate in your own garden. Change your mindset from thinking of them as weeds to naturally abundantly growing leaves for you to eat. Only eat the young ones so keep picking them or cut them back. Over time you will master the art of picking them without being stung by using your fingers like tweezers as you hold the leaves. If it is too much, buy dried nettle but here are some amazing properties that might inspire you to pick you own:

- Nettles counteract dampness, drain water and are a great tonic, cleansing the body of toxins.

- Their vitamin C content ensures iron is absorbed properly and they are rich in magnesium, calcium, chromium, potassium, phosphorus and zinc.

- Nettles have been shown to reduce histamine production and so are good for hay fever. It has been known that a detox in spring reduces hay fever symptoms in the summer.

# The 24-Hour Spring Guide

**Your 24-Hour Weekly Programme — Contents, What to Do with Them and When to Eat Them!**

Start your Rebalance programme at your evening meal. If you normally have a mid-afternoon snack, then still have that. Bold items are your drinks/food.

## Evening Meal

Evening Soup – heat and enjoy ideally by 6pm. No later than 7pm.

Drink 1 mug of warm water if you are still hungry after your evening meal. Stop drinking and eating after 8pm.

**Breakfast –** brush tongue and teeth before drinking or eating, then drink 1 mug of warm water.

**Citrus oil drink/Apple and oil –** stir in the oil so it is mixed in with the juice. For the apple, first warm in a pan then serve in a bowl and pour on the oil.

Then sip 1 mug of warm water.

After 1 hour *if* you are hungry, have your **nettle tea**. You may not need this until late morning.

**Mid-morning snack –** if you have a headache then drink water, try to do some light exercise and/or rest. See Chapter 9 for 'My Rescue Plan *if* I Get Hungry or Have a Headache'. Check that you are not on the turning point of your pancreas going into the low phase (see 'The Daily Rhythms of Your Internal Organs' – Chapter 9); you may just need to rest whilst your body changes gear and it will pass. Your mind will trick you into thinking this is only going to get worse but stay with the process of trying all three (drinking, resting and light exercise) and in most cases it passes. Again, if you are still hungry before lunch then have your **potassium broth**. You can drink as much as 3 mugs of water before lunch if you like.

At lunchtime if you are hungry, have your **soup**. This may be sufficient but if you are still hungry, have your lunch. This is a key time for you to connect to your body's wisdom; ask yourself: 'What do I feel like eating?' Our digestive enzymes are at their highest at lunchtime so eat well and try to keep your evening meal light. You may find you are satisfied with a much smaller amount at lunchtime and in the evening, this is your body rebalancing the volume of food. Or you may find you have a smaller lunch and a snack in the afternoon and then a lighter evening meal. Have your second nettle tea between 3pm and 5pm when your bladder is at its peak phase to complete your rebalance period. Ensure you stop eating and drinking after 8pm. The next day you may find you are surprisingly less hungry than usual as your body rebalances.

# Chapter 8

# Summer

*'Your Body's Many Cries for Water'*

*– F. Batmanghelidj*

# The Summer Rebalance Programme

Summer brings us the warmth and sun we all enjoy, energising us and lifting our spirits. We can ride this wave and feel nurtured from just being outside in the fresh air and sunlight thereby reducing the need to eat food. During the other months we find there is often a need to eat food to keep us warm: in the winter, during the transitional period of autumn and finally the awakening period of spring. In the summer, however, just drinking liquids can satisfy your appetite and lead you to new levels of awareness of your internal body. This helps build up your awareness of your body's wisdom on what foods are best for you and connects you to your **appropriate** appetite. This programme really emphasises that the evening meal is much better for us if it is kept light, and you may find you are eating a lot less at this time of day on your 'normal' days too.

## The Summer Programme

The Rebalancing Your Diet programme for the summer months emphasises only drinking liquids on your rebalance day, which replace your evening meal and breakfast. These are **not** replaced with **juiced** fruit and vegetables but with:

1. **Grated** fruit and vegetables which are then **soaked** for the liquid **only** to be drunk,

2. Slowly simmered leaves and vegetable skins for **all** the nutrients to be absorbed and creating a warm drink if the weather turns chilly or your system is very weak and,

3. Chewed and then **drunk** vegetables, **removing** the cellulose so that you are only drinking a liquid.

These alternative methods reduce the GI level of the liquids and make the nutrients even more easily absorbed. Chewing and removing the cellulose helps us establish better chewing habits when we are eating during the rest of the week, and also mixes the liquid with more saliva so that you digest it more easily. It also satisfies the desire to chew when you are **only** drinking liquids. Often our body gives us a message of hunger when in fact we only need to do the act of *chewing* to satisfy this desire. Remember this is **only** on your rebalance day. When you are eating during the remainder of the week you may find you chew your food better and enjoy your food more. When using this grating method, after draining the liquid and drinking, the remains can be used in a salad or eaten later with another fruit or vegetable.

This programme may seem quite different, especially chewing and removing the cellulose, but most people find they need far fewer vegetables and leaves than expected to feel satisfied. Be open to a new experience. Use vegetables that are quite 'woody', stalks, stems or vegetables such as celery which naturally have a lot of cellulose. Avoid soft fruits as they have a high GI and can be too easily swallowed.

Drinking plenty of water keeps you hydrated and awakens your thirst reflex. A thin soup that you can **drink** may be all that you need for you to substitute your meals on your rebalance day. You may quite quickly discover new levels of energy and a loss of hunger after adjusting your appetite and hydrating your body. If you are hungry remember the three-step rescue plan of drinking water, light exercise and resting as described in 'My Rescue Plan if I Get Hungry or Have a Headache' in Chapter 9. As you apply this process you may find that when you feel hungry your body needs fresh air. All your liquids are alkaline forming to rebalance your body's pH levels and help support your immune system. The liquids also have very low GI levels to maintain a stable blood sugar, reducing hunger and cravings and rebalancing your body's microbiome.

## Regular Routine for the Summer

Applying this process regularly, once a week over the summer months can build up your immune system, clear your digestive tract and rebalance your microbiome. It also strengthens your understanding and belief that you can **raise** your blood sugar levels by drinking water, doing some **light** exercise and resting, as you are giving your body the chance to get the energy from the glycogen in your muscles or fat stores in your body. Or raise your energy levels as your body really needs water or fresh air in order to do this and not food. After a few weeks your body may start to anticipate this period making your rebalance days easier.

## Taking It a Step Further

Once you have completed a few weeks of the initial summer programme and you feel ready to take it a step further, you may prefer to repeat the process for 48 hours instead of 24 hours. What is more important is that you maintain the **regular** routine throughout the summer months. This helps your body get into a rhythm which means it can then start to **anticipate** the Rebalance programme and utilise it more effectively. You are also able to cherry pick new ways of eating that you can build into the rest of the week. Once summer is over and autumn emerges you can then start your autumn programme.

## Moon Phases

The waning and waxing Moon has the **least** effect during the summer months so you may not notice much difference through the cycle of the Moon. However, you may feel during some weeks you get a bigger reaction, for example, you may feel a surge of energy or a headache or increased tiredness. In extreme cases you can feel as if you are getting a cold. This is why I emphasise taking it step by step. Maybe try the first level for a whole month before increasing the rebalancing period. Also allow yourself two steps forwards and one step backwards to ensure **long-term** progress. Once you get the hang of things you may want to increase the length of time you have just liquids on a *full* moon, which is the peak phase of your body to absorb, so you absorb more from the liquids than you would do at other times of the month, thereby satisfying you more. Then return to your normal length of time of 24 hours on liquids for the remainder of your rebalance days. Remember you can have your usual lunch when coming out of your rebalance period if you feel hungry.

If you do end up getting a cold, remind yourself that illness sometimes is not just about fighting off an infection, it can also be a vehicle for your body to release emotional stress, so treat it as an opportunity to really rest and recuperate your energy.

## Getting Out of the Downward Spiral

When we eat something which hits the 'too much' scale on all three pillars, that is, too dehydrating, too high GI and too acid forming, it takes our body out of balance. Our body will do its best to tell us what we need to do to get us back into balance. However, we often misread the messages due to our social habits, belief systems and our addiction to certain foodstuffs. So, for example when we eat something like crisps, fruit bars or cereal, our body gives the message 'I am thirsty' but we often misread it as 'I am still hungry' and we eat more of the high GI, dehydrating and acid-forming foods and the cycle repeats itself. We then get into a downward spiral and probably are not aware of it until it's too late. The Rebalance programme for the summer months helps you turn around and spiral out of it by rehydrating with low GI foods which are alkaline forming.  If you find yourself eating crisps for example, during the rest of the week you may start to notice the effect they have on your body, e.g., overstimulating your taste buds, or you may find them too dehydrating.

# The 24-Hour Summer Guide

**Your 24-Hour Weekly Programme — Contents, What to Do with Them and When to Eat Them!**

Start your Rebalance programme with your evening meal. If you normally have a mid-afternoon snack, then have that still. Bold items are your drinks/food.

## Evening Meal

**Evening juice of grated apple and pear/carrot** – enjoy ideally by 6pm. No later than 7pm.

If you are still hungry chew your **vegetables/leaves** and swallow the *juice* only, removing the cellulose.

Drink 1 mug of warm water only *if* you are still hungry after your evening 'meal'. Stop eating and drinking all liquids after 8pm.

**Breakfast –** brush tongue and teeth before drinking or eating, then drink 1 mug of warm water.

### Juice of grated apple and celery

Then sip 1 mug of warm water.

After 1 hour *if* you are hungry, have your **potassium broth/alternative drink**. The potassium broth needs to be heated up and you have the option of adding salt to taste.

**Mid-morning snack –** if you have a headache then drink water, try to do some light exercise and/or rest.  See Chapter 9 for 'My Rescue Plan *if* I Get Hungry or Have a Headache'. Check that you are not on the turning point of your pancreas going into the low phase (see 'The Daily Rhythms of Your Internal Organs' – Chapter 9); you may just need to rest whilst your body changes gear and it will pass. Your mind will trick you into thinking this is only going to get worse, but stay with the process of trying all three (drinking, resting and light exercise), and in most cases it passes. If you are still hungry before lunch, then have your **vegetables/leaves**. You can drink as much as three mugs of water before lunch if you like.

At lunchtime if you are hungry, have your **salad and quinoa**. This may be sufficient for your lunch but if you are still hungry, have your lunch. This is a key time for you to connect to your body's wisdom, ask yourself 'What do I feel like eating?' Our digestive enzymes are at their highest at lunchtime so eat well and try to keep your evening meal light. You may find you are satisfied with a much smaller amount at lunchtime and in the evening, and this is your body rebalancing the volume of food.

Or you may find you have a smaller lunch and a snack in the afternoon and then a lighter evening meal.  Ensure you stop eating and drinking by 8pm.The next day you may find you are surprisingly less hungry than usual as your body rebalances.

# Chapter 9

## Overcoming the Challenges to Changing Your Diet

*Figuring out your ideal diet is like putting a jigsaw together.*
*Once you find the 4 corners the rest is easier*

You have discovered the four corners of the jigsaw (oxygen, water, pH levels and balancing your GIs). This chapter gives you the remaining pieces of the jigsaw.

## Going With the Flow

I have organised the book so that this chapter contains all the reference material you will need to refer to during your rebalance days. As we are covering four seasons in this book, please refer to the relevant season that you are in.  However, you may want to do the Winter Rebalance Programme during the summer if you are recouping from an illness or have very low energy. Or do the Spring Rebalance Programme in the summer if you particularly want to emphasise a detox process in your body.

Use this book as a reference guide as you travel through the seasons. You may want to reread Chapter 4 at the beginning of each season to help crystallise your understanding.

Please see the Contents page at the beginning of the book for page numbers and full listing.

# My Rescue Plan *if* I Get Hungry or Have a Headache

Please note this rescue plan is for your 24-hour rebalance period. If you are hungry during the remainder of the week at a **mealtime**, then this *is* the time to eat!

Your Rescue Plan if you are hungry on your Rebalance 24-hour period:

1. Try drinking water first.

2. Do some light exercise, go for a walk, if you have energy jump on a trampoline, go for a bike ride, or have a swim. Remember, light exercise *raises* your blood sugar level. I would do no more than 30 minutes (and at least 10 minutes) as you are aiming to raise your blood sugar and oxygenate your cells. It is not an exercise plan to get yourself fitter! Remember the aim is to rest your digestion and rebalance your diet.

3. Go to sleep or lie down and rest. Use the throat smile technique (see Chapter 9 'The Throat Smile') to really quieten down your body. Sometimes your body just needs resources to regenerate cells and clear the toxins out: simple rest gives this to your body without you eating food.

4. Check your body's rhythm see The Daily Rhythms of Your Internal Organs in Chapter 9. Have you got to a lull phase? Will it pass soon?

5. If you are unable to do light exercise or rest or this does not replenish you, try a nettle tea, a broth or a thin soup.

6. If it is getting a bit much it is OK to have a few slices of vegetables or leaves. This fine rebalancing of your diet is not about stressing the body. Remember, your body will still do some rebalancing even if you eat alkaline-forming foods.

7. Have a backup plan for any uncomfortable hunger. Give yourself meals still but aim to have alkaline-forming foods where possible.

## Steppingstones

If the morning phase is too challenging, try substituting *just* your evening meal with only drinks or soup instead of doing the two meals (evening meal and breakfast). This can still give your body the chance to rebalance as it is during the *night* that your body naturally detoxifies. In the morning you could then have your usual breakfast. If your body is depleted this can be more effective in some cases.

Remember you are rebalancing your diet to feel great. If you feel really bad, you are losing the positive effect and you may abandon the whole thing. Allow yourself to have another go some other time or try eating something light. Allow yourself a choice.

## My Story

When I first started my Rebalance programme, hunger used to be uncomfortable. I wanted to satisfy it with food, and I did so initially with very small amounts of vegetables, experimenting with foods that gave me the minimum effect on my blood sugar levels. After a few years of rebalancing weekly when I get hungry now it is a good feeling, and during the week at mealtimes, I can enjoy my food more with lots of digestive enzymes which improves my absorption.

Feeling hungry can be a healthy experience. But if the hunger comes from the unhelpful bacteria within us, we are really feeding them rather than us. Once these unhelpful bacteria start to die off you get to feel the real you! Some people have no hunger at all when they have their rebalance day. They simply do not have the desire to eat. However, it is important you eat during the rest of the week at appropriate times to ensure you get your basic food requirements and hopefully improve your digestion.

# The Daily Rhythms of the Organs

| Organ | High Phase ** | Turning to Low Phase ** | Suggestions for *high* phase: (unless otherwise stated) |
|---|---|---|---|
| Stomach | 7am-9am | 9am-11am | Good time to eat if you are hungry but drink water **first**. **Y**our body needs rehydrating after the drought through the night. |
| Spleen and Pancreas | 9am-11am | 11am-1pm | Avoid carbohydrates between the *low* phase. If hungry try drinking water and see if this shifts the hunger, rest if you can or exercise to raise blood sugar level. |
| Heart | 11am-1pm | 1pm-3pm | Exercise! This also raises blood sugar levels and reduces hunger. |
| Small intestine | 1pm-3pm | 3pm-5pm | Rest as best you can in our climate with no siestas. Have a good restful lunch taking time to eat! |
| Bladder | 3pm-5pm | 5pm-7pm | Drink liquids, caffeine free is essential. This also reduces hunger in the evening. |
| Kidneys | 5pm-7pm | 7pm-9pm | Drink as much as you like before your evening meal. Do some light exercise after your evening meal, if you feel like it. |
| Circulation* | 7pm-9pm | 9pm-11pm | Hot baths are good if you are cold or light exercise if you feel like it. Stop eating and drinking |
| General energy Accumulation* | 9pm-11pm | 11pm-1am | Hopefully feeling rested and ready for bed. If not yoga/ meditation, reading. |
| Gall Bladder | 11pm-1am | 1am-3am | Hopefully you are asleep, but if not allow the creative thoughts! |
| Liver | 1am-3am | 3am-5am | Hopefully you are asleep, but if not allow the creative thoughts! |
| Lungs | 3am-5am | 5am-7am | Hopefully you are asleep, if not then you could get up early and rest some other time in the day. |
| Large Intestines | 5am-7am | 7am-9am | Rise and empty bowels. Drink water, warm water if you are cold. |

* These are not organs in western medicine but are seen as such in Chinese medicine.

** Times are in British Summer Times.

Use this to help you guide yourself back to a **few** of the rhythms of your internal organs. You get easy gains if you start with your liver and stomach phases. Your liver needs to be free from digesting food at 1pm in the morning so this is why we aim to eat lightly and ideally before 7pm. When you are on your 24 hour rebalance you are *aiming* to align with all of them. However it is difficult to follow them all throughout the whole week in our life-style today.

**Food Diary**          Start Date:

This can be a typical three day period or over your 24 hour rebalance period, but still complete at least three days. If you had an unusual day then complete 4 days  Remember to include *all drinks*, with **approximate** time and quantity.

| | Food: | *All* Drinks & quantity | Comments |
|---|---|---|---|
| **Day 1** | | | |
| Breakfast: **approx.** time: | | | |
| Morning snack | | | |
| Lunch: **approx.** time | | | |
| Afternoon snack | | | |
| Evening meal: **approx.** time | | | |
| Evening snack | | | |
| **Day 2** | | | |
| Breakfast: **approx.** time: | | | |
| Morning snack | | | |
| Lunch **approx.** time | | | |
| Afternoon snack | | | |
| Evening meal: **approx.** time | | | |
| Evening snack | | | |

| | Food: | *All* Drinks & quantity | Comments |
|---|---|---|---|
| **Day 3** | | | |
| Breakfast: **approx**. time: | | | |
| Morning snack | | | |
| Lunch: **approx**. time | | | |
| Afternoon snack | | | |
| Evening meal: **approx**. time | | | |
| Evening snack | | | |
| **Day 4** | | | |
| Breakfast: **approx**. time: | | | |
| Morning snack | | | |
| Lunch: **approx**. time | | | |
| Afternoon snack | | | |
| Evening meal: **approx**. time | | | |
| Evening snack | | | |

# The Throat Smile

I developed this whilst I was pregnant and preparing for the birth of my first child. I found it invaluable! It is very similar to 'the whispered ah' if you have ever come across this in your Alexander Technique experience. I have emphasised the smile at the back of the throat as it helps open up your pelvis more and brings the breath deeper. As the breath begins to deepen, this helps stimulate the parasympathetic system and promotes our great relaxing hormones. In fact, there is a nerve that directly connects your diaphragm to your brain and helps bring calmness throughout your whole body via the hormonal system. This helps you feel more grounded, enabling you to digest your food more easily and avoid overeating.

You can do this anywhere in any position, so it is very versatile. I do it many times whilst practicing yoga and in shopping queues or when driving.

**Throat Smile – the Process**

When you breathe out, let your jaw drop open and think of a smile at the back of your throat as you let the air out of your mouth. You may notice a kind of 'ah' sound, which is fine but do not try to force this sound. Any sound is OK, it is just where you are with your body. At the end of the out breath, close your mouth and let the air come in through your nose. Remember that your diaphragm draws the air into your lungs rather than you sucking it in with your nose. Repeat about five times, no more than ten. After a few minutes of breathing normally in and out through your nose, you can return to some more throat smiles. This procedure may begin to change your 'normal' breath into something that is deeper and longer. You can also try some really big jaw opening sessions (like you are doing a big yawn. I would suggest not doing this in the shopping queues!). This helps open up your body quickly and gets more air into your lungs.

If you are doing this in a semi-supine position, you may want to really breathe out and wait for the in breath to happen more of its own accord. This helps lengthen your breathing.

**Quick Guide to the Throat Smile**

On your **out** breath let your jaw drop open.

Think of a smile at the back of your throat.

Let the air out of your mouth.

On the **in** breath close your mouth and let the air come in through your nose.

Repeat 5 to 10 times.

**What Happens in Practice When Doing Throat Smiles**

You may find yourself sucking in the air. Stay with the process and soon you will be doing less sucking in and more allowing. This is why you should stop after several times; we want to avoid any hyperventilation!

How can you do it in a shopping queue? You make the out breath softer, just slightly drop your jaw so it does not look like you are yawning (although I think it is OK to yawn in a shopping queue!). No one will notice you are doing it! If you are still worried, avoid dropping your jaw – just breathe **out** through your nose instead but *still* do the thinking of the smile at the back of your throat; this becomes more of an inner throat smile.

# The Link Between Food and Nurturing

## What Is this Link between Nurturing and Food All About?

Food nurtures you – there is no doubt about that, but you can be nurtured by many other things too: a hot bath in the winter, sleep in the afternoon, sitting out in the sun and resting, catching your breath. When you see a lamb separated from its mother in distress, upon the reunion the lamb goes straight to the mother's nipple for reassurance. The key thing here is ***not to get distressed*** when you are on your Rebalance Programme. You need to go steady with yourself and be able to say no in a calm way to the demands of life, so you can look after yourself better. Organise your rebalance day so you do not get overwhelmed. This can be good practice for some people to apply throughout their whole week, so they can eat well and not be knee jerked into an automatic response to grab a biscuit or coffee when they are in distress. People often misread themselves, thinking they need sugar when in fact they need emotional reassurance. Their nurturing needs can be met by other methods, or they may just be thirsty. If you really feel that you need more nurturing when on your rebalance day, try giving yourself another method of nurturing like a hot bath, a sleep or just resting to catch your breath. Remember, a lot of the time we are just thirsty and not hungry. Try water first or water infused with lemon rind, mint or fennel leaves.

When you are on your Rebalance Programme you find you do not need to cook as much so you have less washing up, less shopping and more time to relax which nurtures you. Whilst you are relaxing you can think of all the money you have saved too!

## If We Overdo It, We Can Lose It

If we do overdo it, we lose sight of ourselves and this whole picture of thinking you need food starts to happen. We are blinkered into thinking the ***only*** thing that we need is food and we have then lost our awareness. This is where the Alexander Technique really comes into play; it teaches you how to look after yourself and gives you the skill of being nurtured by breathing. This technique, that I call 'throat smile', can be used to help you collect yourself and be nurtured by your breath. See Chapter 9 for 'The Throat Smile' procedure.

## The Transition

As you begin to eat more alkaline-forming foods you may begin to feel calmer, clearer and have raised spirits. You may also find you have a greater choice of how to nurture yourself with methods other than food.

When you lose your rhythm of eating well, and you will, it's part of being human, you will gradually establish a link in your brain that says, 'Oh I need nurturing, well I can do this by breathing, drinking water, going for a walk in nature, having a bath *or* eating food'. In the early stages, there will be times when you go straight for food without thinking. This will occur less and less as you regularly apply this programme.

Do not expect this craving to go away overnight! Learn to manage it and become friends with it. You will then be able to watch it and feel the effects. This brings greater awareness and more choice for the next time it happens. As you choose a new route, say you went for a walk in nature instead of eating something, this whole new picture will start to emerge and get stronger in you, allowing you to be able to choose more clearly what your body actually wants, even when you start to lose it!

## My Story

Through my regular practice of rebalancing, I realise that exercise actually reduces hunger, increases blood sugar levels and energises the brain with oxygen. At the end of the day when I pick up the children from school, they tuck into their 'after-school snack' while I drive us back home. If I have paced myself badly, I sometimes feel hungry and tired. With this new knowledge of the effects of exercising when hungry, even though I may be in two minds between eating or exercising, I more often decide to drink water whilst driving and upon arriving home I go for a short 10-minute walk. When I get back, I feel refreshed and not ravenous for food, enabling me to cook the evening meal without snacking and enjoy my meal with a healthy appetite.

## The Microbiome and the Nurturing Link with Food

There have been discoveries of bacteria in our gut that can change the way we behave. Experiments have demonstrated that certain bacteria can cause us to be more aggressive and others to be calmer. As we apply this Rebalance Programme, it will start to address the gut microflora and produce more of the bacteria that generate calmer behaviour. This will in turn help us to make better choices that benefit us in the long run. This links in with the alkaline/acid balance in our diet and how it affects our emotions. Some of you may be thinking, 'That's what I need, a probiotic tablet with the bacteria that calms my emotions.' You do not have to go and start buying certain probiotics from the health food shop: you can address the problem in your **food**. Thinking we can get it in a pill is the old reductionistic approach which does not benefit us in the long run. Bacteria need the right environment to live in and the pill will not create this. This may be just the tip of the iceberg and we really need to address the issue of reclaiming our food chain rather than thinking we can obtain what we are missing from a pill. This is exactly the benefit of this Rebalance Programme which helps you become familiar with alkaline-forming and low GI meals that you can eat over the remainder of the week.

# Balancing Your Stomach Acid

Your stomach secretes hydrochloric acid, but the pH of your stomach isn't necessarily the same as the pH of the acid! The pH of your stomach varies, from 1–2 up to 4–5. When you eat, the stomach releases proteases and hydrochloric acid to aid digestion. By itself, the acid doesn't really do much for digestion, but the proteases that digest proteins works best in an acidic or low pH environment, so after a high-protein meal, your stomach pH may drop to as low as 1 or 2. However, buffers quickly raise the pH back to 3 or 4. After the meal has been digested, your stomach pH returns to a resting level of about 4 or 5. Your stomach secretes acid in response to food, so first thing in the morning you can expect a slightly acidic stomach pH, but not an acidic level representative of pure hydrochloric acid.

### Antacids

If you are taking antacids these could cause an imbalance further down the digestive tract and so it is not advisable to keep taking them in the long run. The antacids reduce the ability of the enzymes to digest food and so the absorption does not take place further down the digestive tract. This can lead to over fermentation of foods which creates more acid in your body. So, taking antacids can be counter-productive in the long run.

### Stomach Pains in the Morning

All this detail helps you understand how you can get stomach aches if you miss breakfast or have some acid fruits like lemons or apples first thing in the morning. Please remember that when the lemon and apple is absorbed it is alkaline forming but, in our stomach, it is still acid. The peak phase of the stomach is between 7am and 9am so it is all ready to produce lots of acid for digestion.

If you already have your general body's pH level which is too acid then it may tip the scales and cause stomach aches, pains and stomach ulcers. Also, being too dehydrated can cause our body's secretions to be too concentrated. So, getting your body rehydrated and alkaline is a key step to alleviate the symptoms of stomach aches in the morning.

## Step-by-Step Guide to Rebalance Our Stomach Acid

If you are already taking antacids to alleviate stomach pain, then it may be advisable to keep taking them until you *start* to eat more alkaline forming foods and *start* to rehydrate your body. On the next page are some guidelines. Individual circumstances may override these suggestions. Keep in mind that you are working towards creating a different *environment* in your body so that the acid levels are balanced again, and you can stop taking antacids.

Suggestions on how to rebalance your stomach acid:

1. Avoid acid fruits first thing in the morning until your body has rebalanced.
2. Find foods that you can substitute for an alkaline-forming food such as eating sweet potatoes instead of rice or pasta.
3. Aim to drink eight mugs of water a day. If you are starting from one cup, then gradually increase this over a two-to-three-week period. Substitute a coffee/tea with warm water. Or try drinking warm water before a mug of tea/coffee. Remember to keep yourself warm over the cold months by drinking warm water.
4. For your evening meal have some steamed vegetables with protein. You could have one meal a week where you just have steamed vegetables or a soup.
5. Aim to have one meal each week where it is 90% alkaline-forming foods. Gradually increase this to more as your body adjusts.
6. Consider reducing your antacids after two weeks. Consult your GP if you have any concerns.
7. Stress creates acid in our body. Try incorporating some routines that clear stress from yourself and/or create an environment in which you are less stressed. This could be going to a yoga class, meditating, or going for a walk after work in some fresh air. Practice the 'Throat Smile' routine in **Chapter 9**.
8. Digital environments create acid in our bodies. Try reducing this wherever you can or having the antidote of fresh air and exercise.

Your weekly 24-hour rebalance will also be helping towards creating a more alkaline environment in your body.

# Rebalancing Your Diet and Immune System

## The Gut Lining and Good Microflora

One of the most easily invaded areas in our bodies is the gut lining. All other surfaces are designed to be excellent barriers to the constant invasion of viruses, bacteria and fungi but the gut lining needs to be open to absorb food. In this way it is important to eat hygienically but our practice of this seems to also block the good bacteria. Digestion is not just a chemical process of enzymes breaking down the food but also bacteria doing this for us too! In fact, it is now believed that **most** infections come in through the gut lining and then reside somewhere in the body.

## My Story

I used to have three or four colds every year, sometimes taking two weeks off work to recover as the colds were so severe. After changing my lifestyle adding exercise and rebalancing my diet regularly, I now have very few colds which last a day or so with just a slight sore throat and hardly any time off work. I also believe the cause of these minor colds to be stress related rather than exposure to a virus. The stress causes an imbalance in my digestive system which leaves me overexposed to invasion.

## Stress and Illness

Stress can cause a huge imbalance in our digestive tract, which needs to be healthy to avoid infections. When we rebalance our diet regularly this gives our body the chance to rest – more so than we would normally. So, when you are on your rebalance day allow yourself to be really nurtured. Have hot baths, go for relaxing walks, take it easy with work, do less, have a sauna or go for a swim. Part of eating is nurturing ourselves and we can do this in other ways when on our rebalance day. Choose your time and day that fits best with this whole process.

For this reason, it is a good idea to do your first few rebalance days on easy days where you have more choice regarding what you can do.

## My Story

When I first started regularly rebalancing my diet, I chose a Friday. I substituted the evening meal with a potassium broth and grapefruit juice; the following morning I did the same with breakfast. I found this easiest as Friday night was DVD night, and I could have a lie-in from the school run on the Saturday!

Once you are in the rhythm of rebalancing your diet weekly you can change your routine to suit the new you.

I now rebalance on a Sunday afternoon, starting with steamed fruit about 3–5pm and then drinking water for the rest of the day. For breakfast on Monday, I have grapefruit juice with garlic and ginger then drink water until 1pm and have a potassium broth, with a piece of fruit about 2–3pm. Monday is my day off, so I get to go for a walk or whatever I feel like!

People sometimes say that some of their nurturing routines on their rebalance day even start to spill over into the rest of the week!

## Seasons

As the seasons change so will your rebalance routine. Find one that suits you. Year after year you will find that it changes too, along with your stronger immune system! Sometimes you may have blips due to the stress in your life or phases that you pass through. Work towards maintaining the routine as your body will get use to this and plan the rebalance routine. Even if it means you end up putting a 'shadow' there, for example replacing a meal with just steamed vegetables. Here is one story demonstrating what I mean by a shadow.

## My Story

I had a couple of stressful weeks and ended up with a slight cold with my period. I decided not to do my rebalance and postponed it for the next week. During the following week I had another stressful time but decided to just have steamed vegetables for my evening meal and for breakfast. The following week I was back into my normal routine. I think if I had abandoned the rebalance in the second week, the third week may have been a struggle.

Your rebalance day is just like exercise. If you do not do any for a while, then when you go back to it the exercise seems a bit difficult, but your body soon gets used to it. In fact, your rebalance day can help strengthen your internal organs just like you strengthen your muscles when exercising. If you have the body type where missing meals is so stressful for your body that it outweighs the benefits, then be happy to have steamed fruit or steamed vegetables for at least one meal. You may find this is fine for your body type and you can still feel the benefits.

This regular routine helps rebalance your microflora which in turn creates an environment for a healthy gut lining. A healthy gut lining also means your immune system has the chance to fight off infections instead of being bombarded with foreign bodies entering an unhealthy, leaky gut lining. Dr Michael Mosley's book 'The Clever Gut Diet' describes this process in detail.

# Your Immune System and Sugar

Consuming sugar can interfere with your body's natural defence system to infection (that is your immune response) and can in some cases reduce its effectiveness by a third. So, if you would like to strengthen your immune system then you could avoid eating sugar. Avoiding sugar can be just as effective as taking Echinacea (herbal extract), which claims to boost the immune system too.

There are lots of steppingstones to help you on the way towards eating more foods that have a lower GI. There are a few listed below in GI order (highest first), so you can have a go at substituting sugar with:

Agave syrup, maple syrup, blackstrap molasses, ripe fresh fruit, sweet potatoes, cashew nuts, coconut products (fresh, creamed coconut, coconut water or desiccated coconut), liquorice tea and ground liquorice.

The lower the GI the less chance there is of the unhelpful bacteria growing too. Once you start this journey then going back to sugar feels incredibly sweet and sickly! If you go gradually, you get less of a sudden detox reaction. If you have the body type and lifestyle to sustain a complete cut out right from the beginning, great – I am not one of those people!

Avoiding sugar not only keeps your immune system steady but also your energy, mood and appetite. If we eat a lot of sugar, then after the energy high we get the energy **drop** and then feel hungry. In some cases, we might feel so low our mental state deteriorates and we get mood swings. This in turn affects our immune system in a detrimental way. This is why on your rebalance day you are eating very low GI foods and so **minimising** any hunger feelings from drops in blood sugar levels. On our rebalance day, our mood may **improve** as we stabilise our blood sugar levels and strengthen our immune system.

## Understanding Microflora and Sweet Cravings

I have discussed this in the 'Balancing GI' section but it is worth repeating again here as we can often be unaware of this happening in the moment. Sometimes when we have cravings for something sweet it is *not* our bodies that crave it, it is the bacteria within us. For every cell we have 10 bacteria! We are, therefore, more bacteria than our cellular selves! So, when we have these cravings, we can remind ourselves that it may not be us but the bacteria in us that cause the craving.

This is why we often are in two minds over what we want to eat. Another good book on this subject is 'The Body Ecology Diet' by Donna Gates. She talks about the big die-off phase where the bacteria start to die off and your body is clearing out the dead cells, in which case you may feel a bigger detox reaction than usual. So, getting rehydrated is again the number one step on your rebalance day. Laying down the steps first means you have less of a bad time and more of a good time! This could also be one of the reasons why we sometimes feel some rebalance days are more difficult than others. If you feel this is a bit of a rough ride, be gentle with yourself and allow yourself as much food as you feel you need as long as it is alkaline forming. This helps you through this stage but still helps your body to rebalance.

# New to Sauerkraut

If you are eating sauerkraut for the first time, I would advise you to follow these guidelines. Note they are guidelines; if you are in any doubt, please do contact me to talk about your individual requirements. You can email me at: hello@integratinghealth.com.

Initially use white sauerkraut (people are sometimes put off with the colour of red cabbage) or use a combination of white cabbage and carrot. White cabbage also has far more liquid in it.

**Level 1** – Drink the liquid only (1 teaspoon a day) at least 20 minutes *before* breakfast away from food. If you do not like the taste, it can be drunk with fruit juice. Monitor your bowels; if your bowels get too loose or windy reduce the quantity.

**Level 2** – If your bowels are OK with Level 1, gradually increase the quantity up to 3 teaspoons of liquid a day ***before*** food. Do this for three days and monitor your bowels. You may need to go back to Level 1 again if your bowels are too loose or windy. If all is OK, move forward to Level 3.

**Level 3** – Start eating 1 teaspoon of the solids per day with your normal meals. Again, monitor your bowels. Reduce the quantity of sauerkraut if necessary.

**Level 4** – Once you are OK with the solid part of the sauerkraut you can eat up to half a mug 3 times a day. Use it as a condiment instead of mayonnaise, tomato sauce, vinegar etc. As you use it as a condiment you may like to progress to red cabbage to add a great colour to your meal.

Peoples' bowels vary greatly. Some people can go to Level 4 after only a few days, some people stay on Level 1 for a year, and some people have it on its own as a snack between meals! Adjust according to your change of environment, the season and time of the month if you are a woman.

**Why do peoples' bowels vary so much?** Your microflora is 'inherited' from your parents, via birth and the first few years of your life. Being vaginally born at home and breastfed by a mother who eats organic food, who has rarely had antibiotics and has a healthy diet, will give you a good start to a healthy internal ecology. This varies dramatically from person to person as the other extreme is being born in hospital, being given antibiotics within the first few days of birth, not being breastfed and having parents who have an unhealthy diet and an obsession with cleaning with disinfectants and chemicals. Getting to know the internal 'weather' of your microflora can be a useful skill in cultivating your immune system. It can take a few years for your microflora to be replenished if it is depleted. It takes five years for a soil to be certified organic as the chemicals are cleared away and the natural soil fertility develops. Thinking long term will give you a good investment into your own health.

## 5 Benefits of Sauerkraut

It is loaded with about 50 strains of good microflora (making digestion easier), cleanses your gut whilst you are eating, has lots of vitamins (including the B group), is a good source of minerals (including iron, copper, sodium, magnesium and calcium) and it has also been proven to affect your mood for the better. Try it and see what you think.

See the Sauerkraut Recipe in Chapter 11.

# Irritable Bowel Syndrome (IBS) and Auto-Immune Disorders

## My Story

When I was a child, I had digestive problems and at the time the term IBS was not invented. I saw a doctor several times who put it down to growing pains or suspected appendicitis. As I had seen the doctor already, when I grew into my early 20s still with digestive problems, I started to seek alternative therapies. I came across Kirlian photography, which measures the electromagnetic field around the body. It showed a disturbance in the energy around my digestive organs. I was advised to see a food allergist who suggested I avoid gluten. This was the beginning of a new journey for me. It was a long and gradual process but it was worth it as I experienced improved digestion, more energy, a stronger immune system and gained my natural weight. Over the years, the food industry started to produce gluten-free products in the shops. This was exciting for me: I discovered other people suffered from what I had which was reassuring, and I could eat bread! However, over time I realised that the other bits that they put in, along with the processing, also irritated my gut so I avoided gluten-free bread and ate rice and other grains that **naturally** do not contain gluten.

Over time, reading many books and sharing experiences with friends and work colleagues, I discovered that gluten can cause the gut lining to be eroded and can interfere with insulin levels causing imbalances in the thyroid gland. This can particularly be the case for those with blood type O.

Dr. D'Adamo, author of 'Eat Right for Your Type', explains that the gluten found in wheat reduces the effectiveness of insulin resulting in a slower metabolic rate and reduced fat-burning.

## Other Blood Types and Gluten

However, even if you are **not** blood type O, gluten *can* still cause various conditions due to the erosion of the gut lining. As the gut is 'leaky' (a gut lining that is too permeable) the gluten enters the body incompletely broken down and causes an immune response. The body starts to attack the gluten particles which are very similar in structure to the hormone that the thyroid produces. It therefore starts attacking its own hormones. Many conditions can arise from this: lupus, ME, an underactive thyroid, anxiety, sleeping problems and many other autoimmune conditions.

## IBS and Microflora

IBS can also be caused by a microflora imbalance. Due to antibiotics, pollution in our drinking water and excess carbohydrates in our diet the bacteria in our gut become out of balance, which in turn causes an excess of candida. Candida is a fungus that is *naturally* found in our gut, but it needs to be in relation to the other *good bacteria* which we often find are depleted. An imbalance in the gut's bacteria can cause an excessive build-up of candida and so contribute to digestive problems like IBS, a lack of nutrition and a leaky gut lining. So we are back to all those conditions that have their root cause in a leaky gut. There are many books on this subject to support this theory, and your regular rebalancing period can help bring your microflora back into balance.

### My Story

As soon as I was born, I was injected with antibiotics as I was bleeding after a high forceps birth. My mother also had an antibiotic injection. Any chance of the good microflora being developed in my body or from my mother's breast milk was gone. Was this the cause of my digestive problems? I feel that it certainly contributed to it.

## Where Can You Go from Here?

If you want to reduce gluten or avoid it completely take one step at a time. If you are eating gluten then start the process of eating alternative foods that provide you with the carbohydrates that you *feel* you need, for example rice (white or brown), gluten-free pasta, quinoa, millet and rice cakes. If this is challenging, then try the gluten-free range as a steppingstone. See how this is for your body type. You may find that you can eat these with no problems. Make up meals that naturally do *not* have bread or flour in them, for example, curries, barbeques, fish and vegetables, gluten-free burgers and sausages etc. Starting your journey can seem overwhelming, but here's a story to help you.

## Barbara's Story (Foster Mother with Three Children of Her Own)

I was size 22 and could not lose any weight. My sister had an underactive thyroid and had hardly any energy. She went on a diet of just protein and fruit and vegetables and got miraculously better. She also lost a few stone! She said just avoiding gluten would help me lose weight – so that's what I did. I have no time for cooking so just bought all the gluten free range in the supermarket. I went down to size 16 without any other changes. I ate gluten-free bread, gluten-free biscuits and gluten-free pasta and still lost all that weight. I am amazed!

Once your journey starts and you see the changes it gets easier as you are inspired to make further changes. We all get setbacks; the key is to remind yourself you can recover and get back on course. When you start to enjoy your body more you find an abundance of creative energy and feel the zest of life again. Exercise starts to feel more enjoyable, and you crave healthy foods.

## Blood Type Os and Carbohydrates

If you are a blood type O then you may find your body naturally works best with much fewer complex carbohydrates (bread, pasta, rice, potatoes etc.) Just eating fruit, vegetables and protein can be much better for blood type Os. We have many food habits, but once we change them, we wonder how we ever ate the food we once did. Your rebalance day will help you find the level that works best for you.

# Establishing a Sustainable Diet Routine

Now that you have completed several weekly rebalances, hopefully you are feeling the benefits. If you can continue this once a week that is great, even once a month can give you some benefits. If this seems too much or you start to lose momentum, here are some tips to get you back on track.

**Keep your evening meal simple just one evening a week.** This helps your liver dedicate more time to clearing out toxins and regenerate new cells (the other main job of your liver) rather than digesting food. If you eat your main meal at lunchtime then you could be satisfied with a bowl of steamed vegetables with cider vinegar and olive oil, or you may be fine with a bowl of stewed fruit.  In the summer, just liquids may be sufficient for your evening meal on your rebalance day and then eat whatever you feel like at breakfast time if you have an appetite.

**Look at *each* meal you have and ask yourself, is it 75% fruit or vegetables?** You may need to devise new meals with more fruit and vegetables gradually. Your weekly rebalance routine will help you get back on track with more alkaline-forming foods.

## Extending Your Daily Rebalancing Routine

You can also extend your weekly rebalance to last a few days. This may begin to happen naturally when you do not feel hungry after the 24-hour period.  This shows you that your body is rebalancing. However, at other times of the month or season you may find that you want to shorten it to your evening meal only. Your rebalance period is when you drink water when you are hungry (or rest and do some light exercise) whereas the remainder of the week you are satisfying your appetite with **food at meal times**, so if you find you are hungry after your rebalance period then eat to obtain your nutrition.

As you go through phases, sometimes extending your rebalance period is easy and at other times you need to break your rebalance period early at breakfast time. This can be influenced by what's going on in your life: season, infections and different phases in your life where you go through major body changes. Life is about two steps forward and one step backward. So, keep focused, and if you lose your routine, you do not need to give it all up; just build it up again one step at a time.

You may consider doing longer periods of fasting, bowel, liver, blood and/or kidney cleanses. Contact a local herbalist or naturopath to find out more information and support. You have established some new routines to help this process go a little more easily. Or maybe this process has given you enough health benefits that you are happy with your energy, immune system and wellbeing.

## Getting Out of the Downward Spiral

When we eat something which hits the "too much" scale on all three pillars, that is, too dehydrating, too high GI and too acid forming, it takes our body out of balance. Our body will do its best to tell us what we need to do to get us back into balance. However, we often misread the messages due to our social habits, belief systems and addiction to food. So, for example, when we eat something like crisps, fruit bars or cereal, our body gives the message 'I am thirsty' but we often misread it as 'I am still hungry' and we eat more of the high-GI, dehydrating and acid-forming foods and the cycle repeats itself. We then get into a downward spiral and probably are **not aware of it** until it's too late. Your rebalance programme helps you turn around and spiral out of it by rehydrating with low-GI foods which are alkaline forming. Also reconnecting to the rhythms of your internal organs makes this rebalance process of regenerating and revitalising your cells a lot easier.

# Other Daily Techniques to Help You Rebalance

Changing what we *eat* helps support our body's natural elimination rhythm, but we can also do other things where we *do not change anything that we eat* and still support our body to eliminate effectively. Some of these are listed below:

**Rise and start your day between 5am and 7am**. This helps your bowels get going and is the peak time of activity of our large intestine. Getting up stimulates your body to have a bowel movement, instead of leaving the unwanted faeces in our body for further unnecessary time. If you do not rise between this time your body may not have a bowel movement until after lunch, a possible extra 6 hours. This may take time if your routine needs changing. Your weekly rebalance of a light meal may help you get to bed earlier and then rise earlier. This will hopefully spill over into the rest of the week. Take one step at a time so you do not overdo it and get too tired.

**Gargle with oil first thing in the morning.** Using sunflower (cold pressed and organic if possible, or any other oil) as a gargle first thing activates the elimination of toxins into your mouth. We often have bad breath in the morning: this is our body's natural method of eliminating toxins. Gargle for 5 to 20 minutes and spit out in the toilet. Then rinse your mouth several times with water and brush your tongue (and teeth if you like). If you don't fancy the oil gargle, at least brush your tongue before you consume anything.

**Drink one mug of warm water before your breakfast**. This helps clear the colon lining of yesterday's food so it's not all mixed up with today's food, reducing further toxins entering your body.

**Stop eating food after 7pm.** If you are hungry after 7pm try drinking water or do some light exercise or at least eat just fruit as this is most easily digested. This leaves your liver to do its daily elimination process in the night and not have to digest the food you ate late in the evening. If you find that socially you are eating late and then do not rise early and have a late breakfast or none at all, you are out of rhythm with your internal organs. Your weekly rebalance can help you get back into rhythm, and it is then like a self-regulating routine.

**Eat your carbohydrates at different mealtimes from protein** (food combining principle). If this is too challenging at least try it for your evening meal. This helps speed up digestion and absorption of food, providing you with more energy and reducing the risk of your microbiome getting out of balance.

**Eat sauerkraut with your meals.** The sauerkraut contains probiotics and can help create more effective digestion of food. If you are buying this, make sure it is **unpasteurised** and has no sugar or vinegar added (only cider vinegar is properly fermented and is alkaline forming). Or see the recipe in Chapter 11 to make your own.

**Try drinking water between meals** rather than having a snack. We are often thirsty rather than hungry between meals, but we too often eat instead of drinking water. If you are still hungry between meals after drinking water, remember the rescue plan if you get hungry (see Chapter 9). Do **not** overstretch yourself as this causes stress on a cellular level and reduces your ability to absorb water and minerals, so if you really need a snack then *have one*.

**Stop drinking (and eating) by 8pm.** This helps your body really rest so it can do its cellular regeneration. If you are thirsty in the night just rinse your mouth out with water so you are thirstier during the day.

# Discipline Versus Denial and Eating Disorders

Rebalancing your diet on a regular basis, ideally once a week, needs to be a discipline not a denial. Denial is something to be avoided as it can lead to resentment; someone's food intake could potentially end up swinging too far the other way causing overeating and possibly leading to eating disorders. Find the balance that works well for you at the time of life you are at. People go through lots of phases in their life and have different motivations. Remember, your body best responds with a *steady* process. Go gently with yourself and allow for the fact that life goes two steps forward and one step backward.

Denial is refusing to give something that your body requests. Discipline is about managing *conflicting* goals. Use discipline to help you rise to a goal of health and happiness getting your health back whilst still *enjoying* your food.

Society is full of junk food, and most food is processed, sugar based and addictive. Learn to eat by some boundaries, which may set you free with health and wellbeing.

## Eating Disorders

Some eating disorders can occur in people when there is a need to *control* their life which they are unable to do. They then route this desire to controlling their food intake instead, as they feel this is achievable. This can lead to obsessive ways as the thing they really want to control is not coming under control. They then try even harder, restricting their food intake even more. This can be *detrimental* to their health. The Active Resting Position (see Chapter 9) is a very useful tool to help control the real aspects of your life that you want to control, or rather *change*. You may then find that you can avoid being obsessive over controlling just your food intake.

Eating disorders can also be related to a tendency of *depriving* oneself of being *nurtured*. As food is so nurturing the control is directed at restricting food intake again. We obviously want to *avoid* depriving ourselves of being nurtured here, but remember you can nurture yourself through other means other than just food. See the section in Chapter 9 on 'The Link Between Food and Nurturing'. The key point to make here is to learn how to nurture yourself and *believe* you *deserve* to be nurtured. If you start to nurture yourself through food *all* the time *and* it is at the *expense* of your health, you have lost your direction. Have a go at nurturing yourself through these other suggested methods so you can fully enjoy life. Or if you have a tendency towards eating disorders you may need to *get additional help* so you can start to believe you *deserve* to be nurtured.

# The Confusion of Conflicting Diet Advice

We are often given advice about our diet without knowing at all where we are starting from. This would never happen with an exercise plan to regain your fitness. Also, our diet advice can be influenced by 'scientific proof'. Unfortunately, 'science' has been hijacked by politics, academia and corporate interests rather than true health for the individual. Our needs change, we are in transition, we need a dynamic solution.

You may make comparisons; however, what makes this programme different from others? Here is one comparison:

What Makes this Course Different from the 5–2 Diet?

• You no longer need to count those calories.

• Your focus is on rehydrating your body – replacing food with water.

• You eat alkaline-forming foods which contain antioxidants, creating a better pH balance for your cells, helping you make better choices in the future, rather than just counting calories.

• You eat low GI foods which stabilise your blood sugar levels, reducing hunger, helping you eat less and balance your microbiome; this again helps you avoid just counting calories.

• The emphasis is on timing to help you eat more in tune with your body's natural rhythms, creating an open door for your body to eliminate toxins more easily and digest food more efficiently; not just *what* you eat but *when* you eat it.

• As you eat like this on your rebalance day you can begin to *cherry pick* your favourite items that you can enjoy at other times, helping you eat well and more easily through the rest of the week too; it's not just about reducing calories for two days.

This last point is the bit where people feel this programme really works for them as they can begin to change their diet **slowly** but still feel the sense of purpose and progress, which is what we are all seeking at the end of the day; that is, **purpose and progress**. The progress is more sustainable and has a long-term approach to improving your diet and health. The key point is purpose *towards health* rather than purpose to *control* something which may lead to eating disorders.

# How the Alexander Technique Has Been Woven into this Programme

## The Alexander Technique Most Commonly Known

People often know about the Alexander Technique as a postural training or relearning process; however, the Alexander Technique is really teaching you a process to help change **any** kind of habits. In F.M. Alexander's books he talks about three case studies: a person with a stutter, a golfer and someone suffering from depression; a diverse range of situations.

Alexander Technique teachers today apply it to just as much a diverse range of applications: childbirth, horse riding, singing, playing musical instruments and actors who use it to improve performance and reduce stage fright. All these examples help people function better, much more than postural training.  At the heart of it is our mind. We are bringing about a conscious change to habits that are often outside of our awareness. In Alexander's words, 'how can you change something that does not exist?' The Alexander Technique teaches you a process to be more conscious with improved awareness. In my experience I came to it through a back problem; I recovered, but then saw the benefits of improving my performance in my job in solving computer problems.

## Applying the Alexander Technique to Food

If you had an Alexander Technique lesson, your teacher would work with reducing the stimulus, quietening down things and then bringing in simple movement into your body, whereby you could let go of the unnecessary tension thereby giving you a **different** experience of movement, one with more ease and poise.  We can apply this to food where we **reduce** the amount of food we eat, consume very low GI foods (so that our blood sugar levels remain stable) and finally drink water when we are hungry (which again quietens down all the stimulus of digestion). We then discover that we can satisfy a lot of what we think is hunger with just water, raise our blood sugar levels with exercise and get energy from fresh air. Please note this is on your **rebalance day** (and possibly between meals during the remainder of the week).  At mealtimes during the rest of the week, if you are hungry you need to eat, otherwise you could be moving towards the habits of eating disorders. See Chapter 9 for 'Discipline Versus Denial and Eating Disorders'.

This sounds too easy and a bit unbelievable. And yes, the Alexander Technique is easy, however, it is the practicing of it where Alexander came into his full light. When you come face to face with your habit you apply the principles. We can get lost in the maze of what to eat when we are hungry and bombarded with information about healthy food and losing weight. Applying **principles** sees you through the maze of changing habits. The three principles that I apply when I feel hungry are rehydrate my body, eat low GI foods and alkaline-forming foods. Why alkaline forming? These are the foods that help our body have the correct environment for all our cellular functioning. If we want to have a clear mind these are the foods to reach for. This is an 80/20 rule, 20% of your diet can be acid forming and this will still promote healthy cellular functioning. See Chapter 4 'The Second Corner of the Jigsaw – Alkaline Acid Balance'.

A lot of the time we really need water, exercise and fresh air or just to rest. If you are then still hungry and want to eat something then use the principles: low GI, alkaline-forming and hydrating food.  Remember this is on your *rebalance day* (and possibly between meals during the remainder of the week).

After people have been on this programme they often say, 'I cannot believe how little food I really need', or 'I did not realise how dehydrated I was', or 'I did not realise I could get energy out of not eating'. Open your mind to a new possibility and *suspend* your current belief.

## Semi-Supine and Your Rebalance Day

If you start to have Alexander lessons, your teacher will advise you to practise the semi-supine position. This is where you lie on the floor and practise the thinking behind your movements. Alexander teachers use the floor as feedback of the effects of our thinking the Alexander Technique directions (thoughts). It also quietens downs the stimulus, so we do not get overburdened. Your Rebalance day is like your own practise of the semi-supine routine. Quieten down the stimulus of eating and focus on drinking water, resting, light exercise and fresh air. You are then bringing about a contrast whereby your body can report changes to you. You become aware of what the food does to you and how you feel afterwards. You get more in **tune** with your body's true needs and temptation starts to **dissolve**.

Not eating is just as important as eating to our nutritional needs and it helps rebalance our microbiome.  See Chapter 9 for 'Active Resting Position – Semi-Supine'.

## The Catch 22 – Our Unreliable Sensory System

In the Alexander Technique one of the principles is that our sensory system is not reliable, in other words it filters out constants. This can be very useful especially if we are overloaded with other environmental stimuli. However, it has its disadvantages too, for example, in terms of our posture, we are not aware that we are slouching when we are at the computer as this is filtered out of our awareness with our concentration on the screen. In terms of food, when we are hungry, we are over stimulated with the desire to eat something and lose the awareness that *sometimes* we really need to drink water, rest or exercise to get fresh air. On your rebalance day you are trying these alternative methods help to **reawaken** your senses so during the reminder of the week you *realise* you may be thirsty when you feel hungry. However, if you still feel hungry after drinking water, resting or light exercise then you need to eat during the *remainder* of the week, so you get your nutrition (avoiding any eating disorders). The key is to not get ***over*** hungry; aim towards ***steady*** changes in reducing your carbohydrates to find the balance that suits you.

## Roger's Story

Roger is a sugar addict with depression who is struggling to get his mental health back and needs to lose some weight. *Excessive* carbohydrate is unhelpful for our optimum microbiome balance and can cause you to put on weight, so reducing carbohydrate in Roger's diet will contribute to improving his microbiome and in turn improve his mental health (and help him lose weight). However, in the *short-term* sugar gives him a mental high, and some respite from his mental condition. He is therefore in a Catch 22 situation, that is, he is in a difficult situation from which there is no escape because of conflicting conditions. His conflicting conditions are that carbohydrate relieves him from his mental condition by giving him a sugar high; this increases the feel-good hormones, but then feeds the bad bacteria and contributes to him putting on weight. So, his hunger stimulation *overtakes* his conscious thinking, and he is stuck in the unreliable sensory perception that he needs that pasty, doughnut or whatever.

Afterwards hate kicks in whereby he starts blaming, including other people. Here you start to define yourself from the past. However, if you start to define yourself from what you do **now**, that is, what you ***do***, ask yourself 'How do I respond to this hunger stimulus?' Or 'How can I be or experience something better than my usual response?" On your rebalance day (and possibly between meals for the remainder of the week) your rescue plan if you get hungry is this: ***drink water, rest, light exercise.***

If necessary, you could also consider eating low GI, alkaline-forming foods which rehydrate; these are not carbohydrates, but vegetables, pumpkin seeds, almonds, quinoa etc. The trick is to be prepared for times when you ***will*** get hungry and have these foods ***readily*** available as this is a ***small*** window of opportunity for change. Structure your day so that you can fit things in and then you are not left in the lurch, where you could leave yourself in a *vulnerable* situation where it is *too easy* to eat the foods that your body may *not* really want.

## The Detail – Our Primary Freedom

One of the principles of the Alexander Technique is also the 'primary control' or 'primary freedom' which connects you to an antigravity system bringing about a feeling of effortless movement or grace and ease to everyday activities. Alexander used this in his application of the technique to change his habits and overcome his condition of total loss of his voice. Using a **principle** to guide you through changing your habits, helps you have direction when you feel ***blindfolded*** during your habits. It is just like a compass, guiding sailors who have no landmarks to navigate with through the seas. I use this on the Rebalance Programme and you will learn how to connect to it yourself. You will then feel in a much better state to make clearer decisions about what to eat or whether to eat at all. When you do come to eat you are also able to remember the four corners of the jigsaw to guide you through ***what*** to eat when you are hungry ***especially*** between meals and on your rebalance day. The four corners of the jigsaw are: rehydrate your body, eat alkaline-forming, low GI foods and remembering that oxygen can give you energy. If you can go through the rescue plan first when you are hungry or have a headache (drink water, exercise or rest), *before* you try food, you may not need to eat anything on your rebalance day or between meals. When you regularly use this active resting position and practise connecting to your primary freedom this helps you make much better choices about food.

## When I Say 'Not Eating Anything'

When I say 'not eating anything', I am not advocating not eating **all** the time; 'breatharians' are not on the horizon here, it is a question of balance and oscillation. We need the contrast to **enjoy** our food, so use it in balance for your optimum health.

We have ***sometimes*** been misled into believing we need to eat certain amounts of food. This programme helps you find the balance for *you* and your current circumstances. Reapply it when you lose it to get yourself regulated again and back on track for your optimum health. The key point is to enjoy the fun of eating (and cooking) but in balance so you can enjoy the rest of your life too.

# Active Resting Position – Semi-Supine

Lie yourself down on the floor with books under your head, knees bent and with your hands resting on your abdomen. You want just enough books under your head so it is not tipping backwards or being pushed too far forwards. This is the semi-supine active resting position (see Figure 1).

**Figure 1 Active Resting Practice**

**This active resting position** helps you reset your body's awareness by quietening down outside stimuli so you can focus on your internal environment in a non-grasping or seeking quality. It helps you start to promote an allowing and accepting quality in your thoughts, a key aspect for you to be able to *let go* of any *un*necessary tension. You can also do this in bed if you are in a lot of pain and need lots of warmth and comfort. Turn your attention to your *out* breath and allow all your weight to drop back onto the floor/bed. Continue to follow your out breath and renew the thought of letting go of your weight. Once you get the hang of it you may find your in breath becomes easier and less restrictive as you let go of *un*necessary tension instead of trying to correct your posture. It is more of an undoing rather than trying.

## Quick Guide to the Active Resting Practice

1. Place yourself in semi-supine position, ensuring you are warm.

2. Turn your attention to your *out* breath and let all your weight drop back into the floor/bed.
3. On the *out* breath think of your neck releasing so your spine can lengthen on the *out* breath.
4. When you find your mind has wandered gently return your thoughts back to letting your weight drop back on the out breath.
5. Remember to undo rather than try.

## What Happens in Practice

Mind wandering! This is natural – treat it like a meditation. When you notice your mind has wandered, avoid beating yourself up about it and just return back to noticing your out breath, building it back up again.

Try it with some movement such as turning your head slowly and see if you can continue to release your neck. Have a go with moving your leg into the straight position or moving your arms to the side. As you practise this active resting position more regularly you can begin to release in activity too, such as in the gym, on your bike, running etc. where you are in a repetitive rhythm.

## Frequently Asked Questions

**Q: I quickly lose the release of my body with my breath and find myself restricting my in breath and shortening my neck again. Why is this?**

A: Habits have the nature of wanting to repeat themselves! We just need to get the new habit *more* established before it becomes *natural* and starts to happen *without* us thinking about it. Be patient and over time you will be able to let go more *quickly* and for *longer* periods of time.

**Q: How long could I practise the active resting position for?**

A: Ideally 15 minutes and no more than 20 minutes as you may start to fall asleep. However, two minutes is better than none. A regular pattern is most effective, just like brushing your teeth, or doing exercise.

**Q: Why do the active resting position?**

A: This semi-supine active resting practise helps you *self-regulate* the buildup of excess tension in your body and reset your body's self-awareness. For you to begin to notice your habits you need to give yourself a contrast. Through the contrast of reduced stimulus and the Alexander Technique directions (thoughts and/or visualisation), you begin to let go of the *buildup* of tension in your body that was **previously outside your awareness**. The floor gives you feedback of your body releasing and you begin to notice your body changing into a more poised, balanced state of being. It also helps you on the way to applying it in activity, reducing unnecessary tension in the moment.

**Q: Why do the active resting position on the floor?**

A: The floor gives you much better feedback than a soft bed, and also you associate sleeping with your bed, and this is an **active conscious** resting practise. You can use blankets underneath you and on top, to keep you warm. However, if you are unable to practise on the floor the bed is better than not doing it at all.

**How the Active Resting Position Encourages Gut Housekeeping**

When we lie in the active resting position, we often get a rumbling in our abdomen. As we release our neck the pressure is released off our vagus nerve which can then function more freely. This nerve coordinates our digestion and conducts the 'housekeeping' activity in our intestines (see Chapter 9 for 'Simple Housekeeping for your Gut'). So, think of it as a good noise that is cleaning your body from the inside. At last, we can do some housekeeping whilst lying on our backs!

I have offered some free resources to support you through this – see the Exclusive Offer section towards the end of this book for more details.

# Learning How to Say 'No' Without Causing Feelings of Rejection

Learning to say 'no' (thanks) without someone feeling as if they have been rejected is an art. Sometimes people have made a big effort to cook something for you and you really do not want to eat it but are unable to say no. This also includes your habits of thoughts where **you** need to feel as if **you** have not rejected them too.

Here are some comments to help you with this process, so *you* do not feel that your family or friends *think* that *you* are being rude or disrespectful when they have made the effort to prepare food or drink for you or they *repeatedly* offer the *same* type of food even though you have spent time discussing that you have, or are, changing your eating habits.

What to say when someone offers you a biscuit:

'Oh thanks for that (as you put it away somewhere). I will have it later as I have just had a piece of chocolate and I'm not hungry just yet.'


What to say when they offer you a drink that they have *already* bought or poured out for you.

'Oh, thanks for that, I will have it later when I have had a drink of water as I am really thirsty now.' Then pass it to someone else, save it for later or, if you really don't want it, pour it down the sink.


What to say when they offer you a piece of cake:

'Oh, thanks for that (as you put it away somewhere). I will have it later as I have just had a dessert at a friend's.'


Over time you could say:

'Oh, thanks for that. I'll let you enjoy it as I have started eating these instead, would you like one?' (as you bring one out of your bag).


Further down the line you begin to *anticipate* that people are going to prepare meals that you will *not* want as you change your diet. You can then start to notify them in advance of your arrival, and they can then start to accommodate your changing eating habits. You may say something like:

'When I come round tomorrow, I was wondering if I could have X for tea so that it makes it easy for you to prepare the meal.'

This way you do not feel as if you are creating more work for them. Or you could suggest you bring a contribution.

 This then gives you an *option* to begin to change without falling back into old habits that you find difficult to turn around again. Your progress then starts to move forward, and you can more easily and regularly rebalance your diet.  You then may start to experience the benefits of longer periods of good health. Understanding this relationship between your health and what you eat makes it easier to say 'No thanks' without *you* feeling as if *you* have upset them.

Over time, you could start to think of yourself as being the leader rather than the awkward one.

# Is Your Personality Tied Up with What You Eat and Drink?

Are you too invested in what you eat because it is now part of your personality, and you cannot give this up?

Changing your *personality* can be *more* of an effort than changing your *diet*. If this is the case for you, then realising this can help you avoid *judging yourself* as a failure or thinking that changing your diet is too *hard*. Believing that you cannot live without such and such a food may just be because you cannot live without this part of your *character*. Once you *accept* this link with your personality and the food that you eat, it can then change your perspective. You realise this is the bit you are not prepared to change. You may then want to say to yourself 'So this is the bit that I need to be *open* to change if I want to change my *diet*'.

You could then ask yourself 'Am I prepared to redefine *myself* for the benefit of getting my health back again?'

'Am I open to the unfamiliar me?'

If you then become more open to a new unfamiliar 'you' then this may mean you are much more open to gaining your ideal weight, or having lots of energy (if you have a health condition of depleted energy), or changing your activities that you do with your friends and family. If they do not want to do your *new* activities, you may then move into a **new** circle of friends over time.

You may then find that things get a lot easier with your new routines of eating, shopping and cooking.

# Simple Housekeeping for Your Gut

When your tummy rumbles it could be your small intestine doing some housekeeping for your gut lining. We routinely wipe down the surfaces and clear up the kitchen after cooking; this is similar to what your intestines do after your food has passed through. The scientific term for this is 'migrating motor complex'.

It is a powerful wave sweeping everything along with it – hence the noise we hear when it happens – which occurs about 2–3 hours after the food has passed through. This is why it is a good idea not to snack between meals – if the housekeeper has not finished, the process stops so that the next lot of food can be digested and absorbed. The sweeping process will also take with it bacteria, hopefully including the unhelpful ones that have recently arrived in your gut and that haven't yet latched onto the lining.

So, avoiding snacking between meals enables this process to happen more frequently. If you find it difficult not to snack between meals try eating some vegetables that are easier to digest and reduce the impact on your digestive tract lining; for example, carrot slices, celery sticks or even sauerkraut (the real unpasteurised version). Sauerkraut cleanses your gut as it passes through your digestive system, so if you find it difficult *not* to eat between meals you could try this as a steppingstone. It can also help lay down the good bacteria for the next meal to be digested more easily.

The term 'clean food' can be misleading as it implies some food is 'unclean'. This is **not** the case; all food, as long as it has not gone off, is clean, but foods vary in their impact on the digestive tract lining. This is just like cooking sausages requires more cleaning up afterwards compared to preparing a few chopped carrots. Some people have become obsessed with 'clean food' which may have contributed to eating disorders. We want to create a healthy balance between eating and not eating. As I said at the beginning of the book, I am emphasising the breathing out phase of the digestion. Please be aware, if we do not breathe ***in***, we still will not survive. It is the oscillation of breathing in and breathing out that is good for us. We need to eat but we also need to rest the eating phase for some internal housekeeping to take place.

Once you have established this *first* steppingstone of substitution and your body has adjusted to this new routine, you could then substitute your veg snack with a drink of water or gaseous nutrition (light exercise such as a two-minute qi gong or yoga routine, fast walking up stairs or even go outside if you can for some fresh air). Over time you may discover that your sensory perception of hunger is ***not always*** reliable. Our rumbling tummy is really our *small intestine* doing its *housekeeping* and we are *not actually hungry*; our desire to eat *between* meals eventually dissolves. However, we are not losing our desire to eat for *excessively* long periods of time. Remember, the oscillation of breathing *in and out* brings about a balance, so we need to oscillate between eating and then resting the eating phase.

Try it and see for yourself; remember the steppingstones so you gradually adjust and get a more reliable sense of what real hunger is, and also *avoiding* any *sudden low* blood sugar levels.

## How the Active Resting Position Encourages Gut Housekeeping

As I said in the section on the active resting position (see Chapter 9) when we lie in semi-supine we often get this rumbling in our abdomen. As we release our neck the pressure is released from our vagus nerve which can then function more freely. This nerve coordinates our digestion and conducts the housekeeping activity in our intestines. So, think of it as a good noise that is cleaning your body from the inside. At last, we can do some housekeeping whilst lying on our backs!

# Chapter 10

# Success Stories

# Success Story 1

# Mary – Unresolved Abdominal Pain

Mary is 60 years old and is self-employed with an antiques business and café. She initially came to see me with back problems, specifically sacral iliac pain; however, she also explained to me that she felt tired through the day, had low mood, was not sleeping well, did not want to interact with people, had no enthusiasm about anything, with heavy headaches and also had long-term abdominal pain. She has had various tests for this abdominal pain (colonoscopy, scans, endoscopy) but nothing showed up. She started reacting to certain foods (chilli, seeds, nuts) with duodenum pain. She started to get this pain four years ago possibly connected to the menopause but also her mother died then too. She had started to take medication 20 minutes before eating to help her digestion.

I asked Mary what she would like from this Rebalance Programme and she explained 'An appreciation of what my digestion is and how my symptoms can be relieved and be independent with it. I want a regime where my digestion is settled, and I can get on with my life. I want to understand how things work together.'

**Mary's typical diet consisted of:**

Breakfast: Porridge with honey

Mid-morning snack: Toast with butter

Lunch: Egg on toast, rice pudding

Afternoon snack: Crackers with mackerel

Evening Meal: Baked haddock, peas and roasted potatoes

She drank 4 mugs of water a day and 4 mugs of caffeinated tea.

**First Step**

I suggested her first step could be to food combine her evening meal; that is, choose between eating protein or carbohydrates, where possible until our first session together.

Mary's first food diary with her first rebalance is displayed on the next page; Mary was following the spring programme.

Here is Mary's feedback from her first rebalance:

'The next day I felt lighter. I got a bad headache at about 10.30am but it went after my lunch at 1pm. I thought I would be extremely hungry in the evening, but I was not. The porridge the next day was more than I needed.'

I asked her to continue with the breathing sequence throughout the week along with her active resting position.

| Day 1 Tues | Food | Drinks and quantity | Any comments on how you are feeling |
|---|---|---|---|
| Breakfast approx time | 7am Porridge | Tea 1 mug water | |
| Mid morning snack | | | |
| Lunch approx time | 12pm Grilled cod and tomato | Tea 1 mug water | |
| Afternoon snack | | | |
| Evening meal approx time | 5.30pm soup | 1½ warm water<br><br>1 mug water | Slightly hungry through the night. 1 mug water then OK |
| Evening Snack | | | Slept well |
| Day 2 Wed | | | |
| Breakfast approx time | 7am Brushed tongue and teeth. Warmed apple and oil | 1 mug warm water | Hungry at 11'ish had 1 mug warm water |
| Mid morning snack | | 10.30am nettle tea. 1 mug warm water | Had a short walk |
| Lunch approx time | 12pm Soup<br><br>2pm Steamed carrot and broccoli | 2 mugs warm water before lunch | Felt hungry after soup. Bad headache before food |
| Afternoon snack | | 4pm Nettle tea | Short walk felt clearer in my head |
| Evening meal approx time | 5pm steamed salmon | 2 mugs warm water before meal | Satisfied in the evening |
| Evening Snack | | Water before bed at 10pm | |
| Day 3 Thur | | | |
| Breakfast approx time | 7am Porridge and honey | Cup of tea | Woke with a headache |
| Mid morning snack | | 10am 1 mug warm water | After drinking water head cleared and I felt 'lightened' |
| Lunch approx time | 12pm Veg soup | 2 mugs water before lunch | |
| Afternoon snack | Oat bar | 1 cup tea | |
| Evening meal approx time | 5.30pm Steamed fish | 2 mugs warm water before meal | |
| Evening Snack | | | |

Over the next few weeks Mary found she could have half the portion of porridge and was often having stewed apple/pear instead.

After Mary's second rebalance programme, she said 'I did not have a bad headache this time and have been sleeping better. I have introduced more vegetables into my diet (celery, broad beans, broccoli and onions) and have not had any pain in my stomach or abdomen and my joints feel easier.'

**Mary's Comments from Week Four**

'After eating the porridge, even though it was half a portion, I felt slightly heavy in the tummy or not as light as I had done. I haven't had any more of it this week so far. I am happy with the apple.'

'I'm having two spoons of the sauerkraut juice probably every other day at the moment. The mood swings are settling down; I don't seem to notice them anyhow. I am not feeling thirsty at all, just sipping the water at nighttime, and seem to be drinking plenty during the day. Stomach cramps have disappeared and the discomfort in my joints is easier. Digestion seems to be much improved, and the almonds are not creating any issues, very delicious and mild.'

Here is my feedback from Mary's final food diary:

With your evening meal of steamed salmon, you could introduce a teaspoon of sauerkraut as there is very little carbohydrate in salmon and your bowel movements are still normal. This will take you to the *next step* of introducing sauerkraut with *food*, helping you digest it more easily.

From your food diary you have had no oat porridge in the morning. This helps you maintain a stable blood sugar level through the morning, reducing hunger and mood swings. If you *ever* do feel the urge to have porridge, give yourself the option of using *quinoa* instead. This may satisfy your need for comfort food *without* giving you a carbohydrate overload. This may not happen for a long time as we are moving into summer; it maybe in the autumn you may feel like this.

From your food diary you only had five mugs of water on your rebalance day, last time you had eight. Even though you had no headache it is still *beneficial* to aim to have eight mugs of water on your rebalance days as this helps *kick start* the thirst reflex for the rest of the week. Over time this helps you get *in tune* with the amount of water your body *actually* wants. Great you felt revived and fresh in the morning/lunch time on Wednesday; you are now feeling the benefits of the rebalance day.

**Mary's Final Food Diary:**

**Monday:**

Breakfast: grated apple and celery

Mid-morning snack: fruit

Lunch: steamed veg

Evening (start of Rebalance Programme): sweet potato soup

Total of 5 mugs of water for the day and no tea

**Tuesday:**

Breakfast: stewed apple

Snack: grated apple and pear drink

Lunch: soup, poached fruit

Afternoon snack: soaked almonds

Evening Meal: steamed fish. fruit

Total 8 mugs of water for the day and no tea. Here is Mary's final feedback from the programme:

'The course was very informative; it gave me a greater understanding of how different things work together, or **not as** the case may be.

The aspect that I enjoyed most was the information I received from the course, which made sense of the symptoms I was experiencing.

The most helpful part was the fact that I could access the information when I needed to and all my questions were there as answers in the ebook.'

Six months later Mary's digestion is still good, and she continues to exercise to maintain a healthy back.

**In Summary**

Small changes to your diet (starting with one day a week) with the appropriate timing of eating (carbohydrates later in the day) and combination (eating protein and carbohydrates at separate mealtimes) can make a huge difference to your health. Mary found that eating fewer carbohydrates reduced the 'stickiness' in her joints allowing her to move more easily which then created a better chance for her to *increase* her exercise and start to enjoy her body, improving overall health. Fewer carbohydrates also help towards a healthier microflora, which in turn contribute towards an improved mood in the long term. These small changes also contribute towards opening the elimination routes so that toxins are cleared from the body quickly and easily, helping her feel refreshed and energised.

For more success stories see www.integratinghealth.com/success-stories.

# Success Story 2

# Linda – Diverticulitis

Linda, a retired financial advisor, suffering from long term abdominal pain.

Linda had suffered abdominal pain for many years and recently had a colon endoscopy which showed multiple diverticulitis (small bulges or pockets in the lining of the colon). She was advised to have surgery and remove part of her colon. She had already had her appendix removed as a child and was reluctant to have the operation. She also believed that the operation may not be successful and felt it was much better to mitigate the symptoms with food. Physically she felt heavy round the middle and eating food was uncomfortable. She wants to avoid sugary foods and be pain free with ease in her bowel movements.

Here is her first food diary. Her coffee is quarter strength caffeine.

Sunday

9.00am 5 fl oz water

Had wine night before and had a headache


10.00am Crunchy bran, bran flakes, oat milk

70ml orange juice, half lemon with hot water

Felt fine


11.30am Americano coffee

Dull ache in abdomen after eating


2.00pm Hummus, carrot sticks, sweet corn, tomatoes, cucumber, mixed leaves, couscous, apple and carrot coleslaw.

10 fl oz water

Dull ache after eating


Afternoon snack

Peppermint tea and coffee

6.30pm Curry chicken, pilau rice (M&S food)

Christmas pudding and ice cream.

10 fl oz water

Large peppermint tea

Dull ache after eating


11.45pm Salted crunchy chickpeas 55g, unusual


Monday

9.00am Crunchy bran, bran flakes, oat milk

70ml orange juice, half lemon with hot water

Dull ache


3.00pm coffee

Dull ache

Baked salmon on sourdough toast. Banana, pear

Dull ache after eating


3.30pm coffee, 3 x 10 fl oz water


7.00pm 1 sausage, broccoli, carrots, pepper, mushrooms, onions, potatoes,

brown rice pudding with oat milk.

Peppermint tea, 3 x 10 fl oz water


8.00pm glass red wine


Tuesday

10.30am Crunchy bran, bran flakes, oat milk

70ml orange juice, half lemon with hot water

Got stomach ache then went to the loo.

Mid-morning snack: Small coffee. Fine

2.00pm Banana, apple, turkey wing. 10 fl oz water, small coffee

Fine

Afternoon snack: 30 fl oz water. Small stomach ache

6.00pm Turkey salad, large salad: hummus, tomatoes, cucumber, mixed leaves, carrots, coleslaw. Brown rice pudding with oat milk

Large peppermint tea. Felt bloated

10.30pm Blueberries and dairy free yoghurt. Can of coke. 20 fl oz water

Stomach ache

## Session 1

I went through the breathing technique and noticed her fingers were moving a lot during this relaxation. I talked her through the 24-hour rebalance guide. Linda also started attending the online stillness class.

## Session 2

After Linda's first rebalance, she said she feels physically better. However, she has picked up a sinus infection.

## Session 3

Linda started to notice a gripey pain when she drank coffee. I suggested she drinks warm water before she drinks her coffee and suggested she reads the chapter 'Rehydrating Your Body'.  I also suggested she use short grain rice instead of long grain rice as this is easier to digest. Linda also started the process of eating sauerkraut following the instructions on 'How to Introduce Sauerkraut into Your Diet'.

Session 4

Linda's head had started to feel better and she said, 'I am starting to enjoy this and will carry on'. Last week Linda said she felt much more positive. She felt tired after the rebalance but wanted to do two. Her reading for this week was the chapter on acid/alkaline balance.

Session 6

Linda reported back and said she is starting to drink less coffee and not notice any difference. Also, she has started to brush her tongue in the morning before drinking water. I suggested this as your tongue eliminates toxins in the morning, so it is a good practice to brush your tongue before drinking and eating in the morning. She is finding she has much more energy.

Linda also started to have quinoa porridge in the morning for breakfast. I suggested this as quinoa is gentler on the digestive lining and has a lower carbohydrate value. At one point in the week Linda had a large meal in the evening with beans, millet, and a cocktail of vegetables and felt bloated afterwards. She felt it was too painful to bend. She also had a vegan yoghurt at lunchtime which she had not had before. I suggested she checks the ingredients of the vegan yoghurt and has a simpler meal in the evening.

Session 8

Linda feels generally much better. She is noticing she is not so tired after the gym, and walking and cycling are easier. She finds drinking water is no longer an issue and feels happier and cheerful. She did get constipated at one point and this makes her mentally unhappy as she worries about her diverticulitis. We discussed a strategy to keep her bowels moving regularly and went through this in some detail as she was going on holiday.

I suggested soaked linseeds, greens, sauerkraut and oats instead of bran. When she goes on holiday, she can take dried parsley or kale crisps (homemade), sauerkraut (as it does not need to be stored in a fridge) and oats instead of bran (as bran can irritate the gut and oats can be eaten without cooking but soaked overnight). On holiday she can have the 'shadow' of her rebalance. I pointed out to her the section on 'How to Maintain Your Rebalance Independently' in the book. Also, allow yourself permission to omit one evening meal, just once a week. This gives your digestion the chance to rest after the big change of environment. Take pumpkin seeds with you on holiday and soak before eating. They are a great snack and can satisfy hunger without compromising the health of your bowels. Develop the mental attitude that you are being the leader rather than the awkward one!


Session 9

I was excited to hear how she did on holiday. She explained she had good and bad bits but fared much better than she had done in the past. Linda had come back with a cough and a headache. She got back on track with her rebalance as soon as she returned. She took a long time deciding whether to do this programme, nearly two years, but said she feels as if it is the best thing she has ever done. She is now back on track and feels great. She has even lost one stone without trying.


Linda really enjoys the online Stillness Class and feels this has helped her find a release in her body. Here are a few of her comments:

'I find my shoulders opening (they felt scrunched up before) and my back is more in contact with the floor. I notice my diaphragm is more engaged and I can fully breathe out.' All this helps her digestion too. The rest and digest rhythm in our body has often been neglected and we find it difficult to switch off. This does not give our body the best chance to digest the food we eat, and it then can cause long-term issues as the pattern repeats itself. Linda has practised this routine regularly and this gives her a much better chance of digesting her food in a more comfortable, efficient way.


Here is Linda's final food diary after coming back from holiday again. She had her usual hay fever that she suffers from at this time of year.


Sunday

Brush tongue and hot water every day

11.30am Late up after being away. Millet, quinoa, oats with oat milk and honey. 70ml orange juice, half lemon, with ginger and hot water

Had headache

3 drinks water, half coffee

1.30pm Rocket, tomatoes, cucumber, smoked mackerel, sauerkraut, kale. Apple, pear.

Afternoon snack: Coffee

6.00pm Quinoa risotto, onion garlic, green beans, peas, cabbage, carrot, bean sprouts, pepper. Three glasses water

Monday Rebalance Day

Before breakfast: Brush tongue and hot water. Missed gym as not feeling good

9.00am Quinoa, millet, oats with oat milk and honey

70ml orange juice, half lemon, with ginger and hot water

Headache

Mid morning water

1.15pm Left over risotto. Coffee, Water.

Afternoon snack: Water

5.30pm Spring evening soup from rebalance

Evening Snack: Soda water with lime cordial (night out with friends)

Three quarters of a pint of water

Tuesday

Before breakfast: Brush tongue and hot water

8.30am Apple oil mix. Half lemon, with ginger and hot water

Mid-morning snack: Decaf coffee and lots of water (to pass time in café)

1.15pm Spring lunch soup (added rocket, quinoa and millet). Did not like the flavour of the soup so tried to change it.* (see below)

3.00pm Three seed deli cracker and vegan cheese. Very hungry. Handful of roasted fava beans. Coffee

5.45pm Omelette with peas, onions, cheese, Spanish sausages (a few slices), salad potatoes, broccoli and green beans. Stewed apple, raspberries, strawberries, blueberries and quark (fermented sour milk)

Wednesday

Before breakfast: Brush tongue and hot water

8.30am Linseeds, oats, pumpkin seeds and oat milk. Orange juice, lemon and ginger drink. Gym

11.30am Fruit scone (at café)

1 pint water, decaf coffee, water. Felt rough and light-headed

1.45pm 1 slice sourdough toast with pâté. Half banana

1 pint water

2.15pm Half coffee

* I suggested asparagus or fennel instead of celery for the soup.

## Summary

Linda said the hardest thing it so be consistent with the water. She may not have drunk enough water on Tuesday (her rebalance day) and felt rough and light-headed the next day. Also, eating out poses a few problems and this is discussed in more detail in the next case study. However, generally she has come a long way if you compare and contrast her food diaries from the start of this programme to the last one.

Three main points are:

- she is drinking less coffee and more water (on the way to cellular rehydration)

- she has stopped eating late at night (helping her digestion to rest and cleanse for the next day)

- she has a breakfast which has a higher content of protein and no gluten, helping her stabilise her blood sugar levels and maintain a healthier gut.

This has given her the experience of feeling more energetic with no abdominal pain and gaining her natural weight. She has done very well. However, this is an ongoing process. The change in seasons can create challenging times for us to adjust our diet. I will be contacting her as she moves into this process through the next change of season and to help her see the changes in gut health through her first autumn where we naturally purge our gut lining in preparation for the winter. This gives us an opportunity to cleanse and rebuild again in the spring. Over the years, if she continues this process, she may find her hay fever subsides along with her recurring sinusitis. We wait to see.

# Success Story 3

# Toni – Menopausal Symptoms

Toni was aged 60, works in an office at a cooperative distribution centre and also as a gardener. She originally came to me with back problems and then later with menopausal symptoms.

Toni had suffered with a bad back for 20 years and had seen various practitioners, but it keeps recurring. Both her jobs have manual aspects as she can also be working in the warehouse in her 'office' job. Her lumbar spine is 'always' aching. Her menopause started 3 years ago. She gets bloated after eating a meal and tries to avoid bread but loves it. Ten years ago, she had IBS (Irritable Bowel Syndrome) possibly brought on by stress. She has had no children and has tried yoga which has helped her back in the past. Her menopausal symptoms include: palpitations at night, hot flushes, bloated feelings, brain fog, mood swings, interrupted sleep and weight gain.

She started my online Stillness class to help her back and after a few classes said, 'it makes me feel lighter and I can feel my muscles release. I can even release my neck during the day.' I kept in touch with her over the years to see how she was doing.

A few months later she got her results back for her liver function and it showed her body was producing abnormal antibodies. After two years from our first meeting she decided to start the Rebalance Programme.

Here is her first food diary:

Day 1

10.30am 2 crumpets with baked beans, small water, aloe vera juice, black coffee, small green smoothie. Still recovering from CV19

Lunch: Felt very emotional, not hungry as had a late breakfast

4.40pm 2 dark chocolate digestives. Coconut yoghurt. 400ml water, still feeling emotional

6.00pm Vegan wings and oven chips, sweet potato with dips. Mug of hot barroca (brand of vit C drink). 4 dark chocolate digestives. Feeling better than previously

Day 2

Breakfast: Jakemans lozenges

10.00am Berry and cherry muesli. Koko yoghurt (made from coconut, dairy free), flax seed mix. Green smoothie, aloe vera juice, glass water

12.15pm 1 crumpet, 4 chocolate digestives. Hot barroca

Lunch: Vegan sausage, cob, onions, red sauce. Immune tea. Felt very emotional

Afternoon snack: Water

7.30pm Chocolate digestives, 3 mint teas.

Day 3

Breakfast: Muesli, almond milk, flax seed mix, banana. Half glass green tea, aloe vera juice, green smoothie. Positive for CV19 still. Feel OK. Blocked nose and a bit chesty

Session 1

We discussed whether she is OK to do the full rebalance as she was still recovering from CV19, but she was happy to do this. I suggested she does the oil mouth wash and brush her tongue afterwards before she drinks or eats anything in the morning. This can help her eliminate toxins without having to change anything she eats.

Toni said she was excited about her first rebalance and she was starting the autumn programme.

Session 2

Toni said her rebalance was 'not bad'. She did not have any bottled water and does not like drinking tap water so was caught out. She did not sleep well on the night of her rebalance due to her stomach gurgling. That day she had a coffee and vegan mince tart at 10.00am even though she did not really want it. This caused her to have her lunch late at 2.50pm and consequently ate her soup later than she wanted at 7.30pm. I went through the daily rhythms of her internal organs which can magnify digestive problems if we eat at the wrong time.

She said her stewed pear and ginger was 'gorgeous' and had that as her afternoon snack too. Her stick of celery that she ate at 1.40pm tasted amazing and I explained that because she ate this as she was coming out of her rebalance, her taste buds are more heightened and her food often can taste more delicious.

## Session 3

Toni was unable to do the rebalance as she was not organised in time. I suggested she focuses on being proactive on water on her rebalance day so she can start to rehydrate her body and satisfy 'hunger' with water. I suggested reading the chapter on rehydrating your body. Until she has got her water filter organised, I suggested she fills a jug of water up and leaves it exposed to the air so the chlorine evaporates and it may taste more palatable.

Toni starts work very early and needs a very light breakfast. She can eat the fruit but does not manage the soup, so I suggested she purchase a food flask to take the soup with her to work.

We looked at what she could cherry pick from her first rebalance that she could do easily for the rest of the week. I pointed out that vegan substitutes often have more carbohydrates such as cheese and sausages which can lead to a gut flora imbalance in the long run. So, we agreed that she could have celery sticks, pumpkins seeds and almonds as snacks as these are low GI and alkaline forming. Toni said she ate loads of chocolate and biscuits and felt a bit crappy afterwards. I suggested she reads the link between food and nurturing in the book to help her gain a better understanding of what causes her to eat these foods. I also sent her the yoga nidra and breathing recording which she can use to help her reduce stress and these 'hunger' attacks.

## Session 4

Toni said her rebalance went well and she did not get hungry. She has not craved chocolate since the last session and has listened to the yoga nidra.

Her reading for this week is the chapter on rebalancing your GIs and housekeeping for the gut. She has started to use the quinoa muffin recipe as a substitute for cakes and bread. She also noticed her bowel movements were not as regular.

Session 5

Toni reported back that she is noticing her hot flushes are reducing and has started the process of introducing sauerkraut into her diet, using the guide on how to do this in the book. Her water volume has generally increased too. She explained she feels the need to buy vegan even though she realises it's not good for her. The quinoa muffins have helped with this as this is still vegan and are an easier protein to digest compared with pulses and legumes.

Toni said she feels positive and inspired for the next rebalance.

Session 6

Toni reported back that she is starting to feel as if she is moving forward. She notices that she feels bloated the day after eating vegan cheese, and the day after her rebalance she feels slimmer. I pointed out that this is the benefit of the rebalance; it creates a contrast so you can clearly see which foods cause your problems. Last week Toni moved on to the winter programme. The next session will be on the other side of Christmas.

Session 7

Toni reported back that she is feeling much more energised over the last 2 weeks. Her bloating is generally better although she can still feel it sometimes. Her bowel movements are more regular and well formed.  She is now on solid sauerkraut in the mornings only. She feels charged and energised for the next rebalance.

Session 8

Toni reported back that she has started to make her own sauerkraut, and that the yoga nidra works well on her rebalance day. She continues to not feel hungry in the evening. She does feel she needs to get more organised and is still struggling with her memory. She realises this is a lot to do with self-worth too. We talked about the sankalpa in the yoga nidra (stating what you would like to resolve in your life) to help with gaining more self-worth.

Toni feels she definitely has more energy and vitality and said, 'the odd times when I eat something that is not good for me I notice my energy drops.' I suggested she reads 'Discipline vs Denial' in the book which may help to avoid this.

From her food diary she drank a coffee on the morning of her rebalance and also ate an avocado and muffin on the following day in the morning as she was out at a café and felt there was nothing else she could have. We discussed a strategy for eating out and how she can ask for her meal to be tweaked to meet her needs. Being grounded when eating out is key for Toni so she feels she can choose what she actually wants. I often say to clients, be the *leader* rather than feel the awkward one!

Generally, Toni's food has changed significantly. Here is her food diary for this week.

Day 1

7.15am Half grapefruit. Mug water, mug hot water with honey lemon and ginger. The day before I had dates and felt bloated. Had a bowel movement at 9.20am

11.00am 1 almond with sauerkraut. 2 glasses water

12.45pm Veg burger, sweet potato chips, roasted beetroot, green salad. Bubbly elderflower

3.00pm 3 almonds

4.20pm Half apple. Water

6.00pm Evening soup. Water. Yoga nidra

Day 2

7.30am Grapefruit and ginger. 2 mugs water. Bowel movement

10.45am 1 nut, sauerkraut

12.30pm Half black coffee (eating out with husband)

1.10pm Protein fix, celery and cucumber. Mug water

6.30pm Nut roast, veg, greens, gravy. Bubbly elderflower

8.00pm Water. Bowel movement because ate such a big meal

Day 3

9.15am Avocado muffin. Mug water, glass water

10.30am Sauerkraut. Glass water

1.00pm Choc fruit and nut balls. Glass water. Felt full and bloated

1.40pm Protein fix – full one. Hot water, honey, lemon and ginger

Session 9

Toni explained she went away and could not take her sauerkraut. She now realises the benefit of eating it as it can regulate your bowels, improve digestion, and has a great taste.

Toni feels she is good at the rebalance now and she does not feel hungry. She is not so regular with practising her yoga nidra. She notices her symptoms go 'bonkers' when she eats biscuits and chocolate, her hot flushes come back. She also drinks alcohol after her shiftwork as this helps her relax. I suggested she has water with the alcohol to minimise its effects and practice her yoga nidra more frequently to get her fix of relaxation in other ways.

Toni continues to report back that the millet and quinoa is 'gorgeous'. This is a great substitute for cakes and bread.

Her brain fog is better, and her memory is coming back which is really noticeable. She has more energy again and if she does eat biscuits she gets her hot flushes. We discuss denial vs discipline again and for her to keep monitoring the pattern of why she wants the biscuits in the first place. I also suggested she could try the alkaline chocolate sauce recipe as an alternative to biscuits as this is less addictive and has a lower GI.

I suggested she could start to eat sauerkraut with her main meal as well as a snack now.

Toni feels excited and clear about her next rebalance.

At Toni's final review session, she described herself as more confident. She feels 65–75% on board with the rebalance. She notices that she is very sensitive to the full moon phase, and it causes her to be tempted by food, so she increases her quantity during this time. Generally, though, her portions have decreased. The days after her rebalance she also feels that she over eats; she thinks this is psychological though. This is during the winter season and things may be different as she travels through the next two seasons.

She said, 'I am really pleased with the teachings and the programme. I realise it is down to self nurturing then I can get the discipline. I am enjoying the cooking and being more prepared each time. I am sad that it has come to an end but also excited to take it forward. It's been so good. I can see so much benefit and how my whole diet has changed not just on the rebalance days.'

Toni decided to continue with the online Stillness class too.

I will keep in touch with her and help her to navigate the transitions through the change of seasons for at least another year.

# Success Story 4

# Zena – Investing for her Senior Years

Zena, aged 59, runs her own business in hospitality in Yorkshire.

Zena would like to regain suppleness and posture, increase her aerobic capacity and build her mind–body confidence. She worries about being a frail woman and would like to be lighter in herself and have more energy.

She tends to eat a high-carbohydrate diet and drink a lot of tea and coffee and hardly any water.

She does not exercise apart from housework. She does not change the beds as she slipped a disc in her back a few years ago and is continuing to recover from this.

I met Zena at a health and wellbeing talk and from this talk she already took on board to drink more water before she started the programme. Here is her first food diary:


Food Diary 1

Day 1 Sat 3rd Dec

1 litre water. Lovely fresh

Breakfast 11am Gluten-free toast with butter and scrambled eggs. Fuelled

12pm Hot chocolate

6pm 1 litre water. Refreshing

7pm Cavolo nero, garlic, salami, salt, pepper Light satisfied

10pm Hot milk. Easy


Day 2 Sun 4th Dec

7.15am 1 litre water

Breakfast: Egg, tomato, mushroom, omelette, 1 sausage, 1 bacon. Full bit heavy

1pm Home made carrot cake. Tea. Light

4pm Tea. Hungry

6pm Quarter of pizza, coleslaw. Apple crumble and custard all from Co-op. 1 litre water. Worried. Fullish

Day 3 Mon 5<sup>th</sup> Dec

7.30am 1 litre water. Fresh

11.30am 2 fried eggs 1 slice wholemeal toast

2 slices white toast and marmalade. Good but induldged

7pm Oven-baked salmon, 3 leaf salad, potato salad. Brilliant. Fresh

Evening: Felt dry mouth. Only drank 1 litre water


After Zena's first rebalance, she said, 'it was a revolutionary experience, it helps me to reflect on how I normally eat. I am really looking forward to having the next rebalance as you cannot go too far back to old eating habits. I am amazed how little I have eaten, and this has not undermined my energy.'


Second Rebalance

At Zena's second rebalance, she did not feel as wonderful as the first, but she still felt good and did not feel hungry.

Christmas came along and Zena said she over eaten the chocolate and cake as it was difficult to say 'no'. I suggested reading the section on 'Learning How to Say No Without Causing Feelings of Rejection'.


Fifth Rebalance

Zena felt she was eating more on her rebalance. I explained that this may be due to the timing of eating, and it is structured so she eats more regularly but with light meals.

Zena observed she is eating smaller amounts in the evening through the rest of the week.

Zena explained to me, 'I feel it is revolutionary as I have never focused on my emotional needs. I am beginning to realise what a powerful thing it is.'

I suggested to Zena to read 'Denial Versus Discipline and Eating Disorders' in Chapter 9. We discussed how she could extend her rebalance and start cherry picking some more things to do in the rest of the week. I suggested reading 'Other Daily Techniques to Help You Rebalance' in Chapter 9.

Sixth Rebalance

Zena continues to realise she can eat smaller portions and sees it's more about self worth. Here is what she said about the breathing technique: 'I am doing the breathing in bed in the morning. This is astonishing as I feel so different afterwards, I feel as if I am rightfully taking my place in the world.'

We discussed how to tune into her body as she runs a bed and breakfast and can overeat the leftovers of the guests' breakfast when it's not really what her body wants. We looked at various strategies of freezing it or eating it at another meal, fully utilising the leftover food to replace a meal at another time, saving money and food preparation time.

See Food Diary 6 below.

Day 1 Sat 28th Jan

7am 1 litre water

Breakfast: Apple, brazil nuts, walnuts, pumpkin seeds, linseeds, quinoa, lime, cinnamon

1.30pm Egg, leaves, tofu. Water. Light fuelled

7pm Kale, broccoli, peas, cauliflower, pepper. Filled and satisfied, light and comfortable

Evening 1 litre water


Day 2 Sun 29th Jan

7.30am 1 litre water

9am 2 Veggie sausages, 1 mushroom, 1 halloumi, 1 bacon, 1 tiny black pudding. 1 cup water. Body registered this to be a bit too much in volume – otherwise fine but not light

1.30pm Omelette – 2 eggs, onion, garlic, pepper and sprinkling blue cheese. Bit rich but not over heavy

4pm Half piece of fresh sourdough with olive oil

3pm 1 litre water. No changes

6.45pm Fried banana with cumin, cardamom, brazil nuts, walnuts, coconut oil

Hot chocolate, coconut oil and oat milk. Realised I have not eaten any greens all day! Happy tummy

Day 3 Mon 30<sup>th</sup> Jan

7am 1 litre water

9.30am Okra, nuts, garlic, coconut oil. Bit strange but felt OK. Started day with migraine for first time in years (poss. 15?)

1pm Egg, spinach, pickled courgette, gluten-free toast. 1 cup of tea. A bit better, some relief in head, energised

Evening meal: Kale and pea soup. On rebalance. Better again, refreshed

8pm 1 litre water


Day 4 Tue 31<sup>st</sup> Jan

Breakfast: 1 litre water

10am Apple drink (Rebalance)

1pm Leek and courgette soup. Filled and light

3pm Protein fix. Light not hungry

3.30 pm 1 litre water

6.30pm Nut roast, cavolo nero, solsify

Seventh Rebalance

Zena continues to make changes to the rest of the week's diet and says, 'Food combining my meals helps me maintain lightness.'


Eighth Rebalance

In this week's rebalance, Zena starts to see how her body reports more to her as she continues her weekly rebalance. She explained, 'I find it much easier to say no to potatoes as I am finding them difficult to swallow.' As the rebalance created a contrast of eating food which is *easy* to digest and *good for her* body when she eats something that is *not right for her body* it clearly lets her know now.

She also commented, 'the yoga nidra is very helpful as it allows me to refocus.'

At the end of the programme Zena said, 'I feel a big difference in my body, I feel more in tune with myself and my energy continues to be buoyant. I even notice that I can now reach the skylight window at home without using a step.'

# Success Story 5

# Cathy – Weight Loss and Improved Sleep

Cathy, aged 52, wanted to lose weight around her middle, get fitter and sleep better as she always woke between 4am and 5am. She has a stressful job working for a housing association. She said, 'I need to lose half a stone and would like to be able to say no to sweet things when I am bored, tired or stressed.' I asked her what her life would be like if she did nothing and she said, 'If I didn't stop eating I would be bigger, annoyed and embarrassed about letting myself go, even my Mum use to nag me to lose weight.'

Here is her first food diary – the tea and coffee are caffeinated

Day 1

Breakfast: Sip of hot water. Small bowl of muesli, granola, brazil nuts, blueberries and Greek yoghurt

10.00am Green tea, half glass green smoothie, mug coffee

12.30am Carrot, celery and lentil soup, sourdough, half avocado filled with cottage cheese, 4 Rich Tea sandwiches with butter. Half mug hot water

Afternoon snack: Mug of tea

6.30pm Mushroom risotto, parmesan and Greek yoghurt, raw spinach

Evening snack: 4 Rich Tea biscuits, 2 dates, 2 Rich Tea biscuits. Hot water


Day 2

6.30am Tea

7.30am Tea

8.45am Small bowl of muesli, granola, brazil nuts, blueberries and Greek yoghurt. 1 mug of coffee

Mid morning snack: Half glass green smoothie

1.00pm Smoked mackerel and hot tomatoes, 1 slice seeded brown bread with no butter, 1 slice bread with butter and golden syrup, 2 Rich Tea biscuits. Cup of hot water

Afternoon snack: Cup of tea

Evening meal: Salmon, green beans, tomato and anchovies. 2 dates. 2 Rich Tea biscuits. Glass tonic water

Evening snack: Hot water


Day 3

6.30am Tea

7.30am Tea

8.45am Small bowl of muesli, granola, brazil nuts, blueberries and Greek yoghurt

Mid morning snack: Glass of green smoothie

Lunch: Celery and stilton soup. 4 malted milk biscuits. Green tea – half mug. Coffee – mug

Afternoon snack: Satsuma. Half hot water. Mug of tea

Evening meal: Chicken breast and chickpea curry. Home-made sauce. Dates. Hot water


Session 1

At Cathy's first session we went over the breathing and the 24-hour guide starting with the winter programme. We discussed water first and how she can start to drink water instead of green tea. I suggested she fills a bottle with water, so she knows how much she is drinking. I also suggested she could aim to listen to the recording of the active relaxation daily. I explained the importance of getting rehydrated as this can reduce the stress response in the body, improve cellular functioning, improve sleep and reduce the hunger levels.


Session 2

Over the week Cathy had already drunk twice as much water and eaten fewer biscuits. Her rebalance went well although she had a light head around lunchtime at the end of her rebalance. I suggested she tries some light exercise instead of a snack during the morning as she may be oxygen deprived rather than hungry as she is sat at a desk a lot of the time at work.

We also talked about having soup (or alternative) for breakfast on the other mornings with a lower GI, and higher mineral content, to replace her muesli breakfast which gives her a high carbohydrate meal. This can reduce the high and low blood sugar levels in the morning.

I explained that the combination of fat, sugar and salt switches off the brain's mechanism to say, 'I have had enough'. So, it is easy to overeat on food types such as biscuits. Eating pure dates may satisfy the sweet craving without the tendency to overeat.

Cathy reported she has already got into batch cooking and slept through for the first time last night.


## Session 3 – moved onto Spring Programme

Cathy reported back that she is feeling more refreshed upon waking, finding it easier to drink water in the morning and is sleeping through 50% of the time now. Her elderly father has been needing support and so Cathy has to travel and stay over. This disrupts her routine, and she needs to establish a new routine there with her father. We discussed how she could do this without upsetting her father; explaining to him what she is doing and why is key for her to feel comfortable with her new routine.


## Session 4

Cathy now reports that there are no biscuits in the house now! I suggested she can have a mug of hot water before she has her tea or coffee each day. If she feels like the tea after the hot water, then go ahead. However, this process helps her gradually reduce the need for tea when her body may really be satisfied with water only.


## Session 5

Cathy reported back that she has started to lose weight and her clothes feel looser. She feels more alert in the mornings and is less tired. On the day after her rebalance she feels energised.

Cathy explained that she does not really like the sweet potato soup and I suggested putting lemon or a cooking apple in to take down the sweetness.

We agreed that her next step could be to drink more water in the afternoon before her evening meal as this can help reduce 'hunger'. Sometimes we are just thirsty in the evenings but misread this to be hunger.

Session 6

Cathy is now drinking nettle tea instead of her usual caffeinated tea (see food diary below). She also discussed her experience of eating late with a badly combined meal and did not sleep well. This helped Cathy realise the importance of food combining her evening meal.

On her rebalance she started to get hungry and so had a proper lunch. I explained this is fine as we are at our peak time of digesting at lunchtime, so to enjoy her lunch.

She notices she is now actually feeling thirsty and wants to drink more water.

She explained she had a 'blip' on Saturday and wanted something sweet and ended up having a croissant, some crisps and chocolate. She felt bloated afterwards but still slept well. I explained that her body is reporting the contrast to her and the regular rebalance period helps her stay in tune with this messaging system. Its great she noticed.

Food Diary Session 6

Day 1

Before breakfast: 2 cups water

8.00am Apple and oil. 1 cup water

10.30am Muesli and yoghurt – almonds. 1 mug coffee

2.30pm Leek and potato soup

Evening meal: Roast duck, sweet potato and green beans. 1 Ryvita and currants. Cup of tea

Evening snack: 1 Ryvita. 1 hot water


Day 2

Before breakfast: Hot water x 2

9.00am Boiled egg x 1. Hot water x 1, nettle tea x 1

10.30am Green smoothie

Lunch: Leek and potato soup

Afternoon snack: Hot cross bun x2. 1 cup tea

Evening meal: Bean, fennel and cabbage stew with salsa verde. Ryvita with currants x 2. Hot water

Evening snack: 6 almonds, 2 dates. Hot water

Day 3

Before breakfast: 2 x water

8.30am Boiled egg. 1 nettle tea

10.00am Green smoothie

11.00am Half apple. Mug of coffee

Lunch: Cottage cheese, avocado, tomato, beetroot. 1 x Ryvita

4.00pm Mug of tea

5.00pm 1 x hot cross bun no butter. Hot water

7.00pm Turkey breast, rocket, tomato, cucumber with balsamic dressing. Hot water

## Session 7

Cathy reported back that she has lost half a stone and feels trimmer. She now wants to lose another half stone.

Her biscuit addiction slipped in the last couple of weeks as she got stressed, the apricots did not give her the fix. I suggested soaked dried fruit with coconut milk or cream and a pinch of salt to get the fat, sugar, salt fix but not in a biscuit format which can be dehydrating and so less addictive. The body may produce the thirst reflex after eating biscuits, but people often misread this as 'I must be still hungry' and end up overeating on biscuits. The key is to be prepared and look at how she can respond to the stress differently.

## Session 8

Cathy reported back that she has started to notice she does not suffer from heart burn as frequently. She has made salads from the 'Eat to Feel' recipe book and says, 'It is remarkable how easy it is to have soup only in the evening and not be hungry.'

Cathy has done well considering her personal circumstances of stress levels with work and family. She has achieved several small steps and maintained these. Small changes repeated over a long period of time produce a big impact. Hence her improved sleep, loss of weight, increased levels of energy and less acid reflex. I continued to stay in touch with her after the programme and here are my notes from conversations on the phone:

Six months later…

Telephone call 1

Cathy said, 'At the end of the summer I was fine, but it had gone pear-shaped since. I am still drinking water and stewed fruit for breakfast but slipped back on biscuits. I went away on holiday and lost the routine. My husband has also been very stressed.'

We discussed some steps to help her get back into her routine and we agreed the evening soup would be the easiest and that Cathy was to read the guide on continuing my rebalance independently.

Telephone call 2

Cathy's Dad had been very ill, her job had changed, and she had started snacking again. I suggested that she start with her evening soup as she found this the easiest to do.

Telephone call 3

Cathy has again been very stressed at work as her colleague is on maternity leave and she has to do all the work. She knows this causes her to make unhelpful decisions around food. At this point I started to suggest other methods to reduce stress and for her to go back to her recordings and listen to the semi-supine or the throat smile recordings when she gets back from work. Make friends with your mistakes and then you can look at the patterns of thoughts more closely. Getting the antidote to the stress first before eating is the key to changing your decisions around food. Also, I asked whether it was possible for her to talk to someone at work? Could they put something in place, so it creates less of a strain on her?

Telephone call 4

Cathy has managed to start a Pilates class at lunchtime and has done a few rebalances. Well done Cathy!

Telephone call 5

Cathy has an improved work environment and is now back doing the rebalance once a week with the evening routine only.

Telephone call 6

Cathy's knee has swelled up and she is seeing a consultant. She said she still has the intention of doing the full rebalance weekly.


Telephone call 7

Cathy has had a knee operation and been off work. She has now been able to focus on eating well and has lost 5lbs in weight. She feels as if the diet has helped her recover from the operation quicker. She is surprised she has lost 5lbs even though she has been limited in movement due to her knee. She realises eating well is the key.


Hopefully Cathy's experience will help her realise when she loses focus again due to stress, that the key is to get on top of it as a priority so she can stay on track with her food. The word priority is the key. The mind often convinces us we have no time but if we use the word prioritise then the important things get done first and the smaller ones sort themselves out.

This is why the semi-supine recording, the throat smile, the yoga nidra and the online Stillness class are such key aspects of the programme. The piece of the jigsaw relating to oxygen is just as important as the other food pieces. Not only can it give you more oxygen to the brain and creates a better environment for your body to digest but it reduces stress so your brain can make better decisions.

Regular practice ensures you do not get too far off track. Making this a priority and a *necessity* rather than a luxury is also the key. That way if you remove the idea of it being a luxury you are less likely to allow self-worth issues to get in the way.

# Chapter 11

## Recipes and Guides

# General Points for All Seasons

## The Energy of Food

There are many different aspects to food than just its nutrients, taste, texture and temperature. Food has many different qualities in the model of Qi energy. Qi is the vital force forming part of any living entity and has been measured with specialised photography. Organic food generally contains more Qi energy than non-organic. Certain foods have an attraction to certain parts of our body. This is a fascinating world to discover and experience. These recipes align you to this Qi energy and your biodynamic rhythms which give them their uniqueness.

## Soups

Soups are made from vegetable stock/potassium broth and **not** from a stock cube. This is the old, traditional way of creating a stock. It draws out the mineral content of the vegetables which is then more easily available for absorption. There are more vitamins and minerals in the skins and stalks of vegetables than in the sweeter tasting centre. It is the use of the skins, stalks and leaves of vegetables that make the difference. With shop-bought vegetable stock **often** the centre of the vegetable is used whereas the potassium broth is *only* using skins, stalks and leaves. This method creates a potassium broth which is an excellent drink to have on its own with a little sea salt, if required, when you are on your rebalance day. Creating this type of stock (or potassium broth) makes soups more satisfying and can reduce food cravings. If you are making a soup for your rebalance day, it is *key* that you make this potassium broth as it will help you absorb more vitamins and minerals, helping the rebalance day to be a lot easier!

Any peelings of vegetable skins, onion skins, garlic skins, leaves of vegetables and stalks can be used. For example, young carrot tops, roots of leeks, celery ends, sweet potato skins, fennel stalks, onion skins, etc. Vegetables to *avoid* are cabbage, cauliflower, sprouts and broccoli as these can produce flatulence. Use organic vegetables if you can and if not, ensure you wash them. On the rebalance days I avoid potato skins as these contain a natural sugar that is very difficult for our bodies to digest. Onions skins can taste bitter, so go sparingly with these.

In the spring, I collect nettle leaves and add these to my stock. In the summer and autumn when the leaves are in abundance, I collect herbs from the garden and add these too. If you pick nettles through the summer, then you get the young leaves coming through in the autumn too.

### *Method for Vegetable Stock (or Potassium Broth Drink)*

Collect the vegetable peelings over a couple of days and store in the freezer until you have enough to fill a large pan. Pour in water, **just enough** to cover the vegetables. I sometimes make it on the fly. As I am preparing a soup, I have another pan on the go doing the stock, I simmer for 20 minutes and then drain off and add to the soup pan. You get about 50% of the mineral content after 20 minutes. You can top up again with water (just enough to cover the vegetables) and leave to simmer for an hour for the remainder to brew.  Or if you are not making soup at the time, simmer over a low heat for 1–2 hours. Once you have made your stock, drain off the liquid and store in a jar in the fridge. This will last for five days, or you can freeze the broth in plastic containers.

### *Alternative Potassium Broth Drink*

If you are out and about and cannot take your potassium broth in a flask, then have a cup of nettle tea instead. This is much more convenient and still palatable if you have to drink it cold.

## General Points for All Seasons

**The Soups:** The *evening* soups can be made using vegetables with starch such as sweet potato, butternut squash and carrot, but complement them with a low-starch vegetable, for example butternut squash and celery, sweet potato and leek, carrot and kale. The *morning* soup needs to be low in starchy vegetables, for example soups with low starch include asparagus and courgette or celery and kale.  Use the vegetables that are in season and organic if possible. To start with you may use carrot in the morning with a lot of kale to introduce your body to low GI foods in the morning, as carrot has less carbohydrate in than butternut squash and sweet potato. Over the weeks and depending on the season, migrate to low-carbohydrate vegetables in the *morning* and maybe eventually in the *evening* too. Please substitute vegetables that you do not like with ones you do. So, for example, if you do not like celery, substitute with fennel or courgettes. Sweet potatoes can be substituted with carrots, pumpkins or butternut squash.

## General Information and Tips on Portions

This is the bit that you really need to rein in. Keep food out of temptation as you will be adjusting portion sizes and your mind may convince you that you will need more! Remember this is on your **rebalance day** to help you adjust, *whether* it be your microflora, water intake or body weight. Please **do** make accommodations if you are a particularly large-built man or woman or have a very manual job.

## Quinoa and Millet

When making quinoa and millet mixture you will want to cook more than one meal's requirements, so once cooked, portion it out and freeze the remainder so you are not tempted to overeat!

## Stewed Fruit

Use a little water to dilute down and use about half the fruit on your rebalance day. It is surprising how little food you need. Freeze the remainder for your next rebalance day the following week or use it as part of your normal breakfast the following day. People often end up eating this as their normal breakfast instead of porridge, toast or cereal, but they often have a bigger portion. Although plums are slightly acid forming, I have included them in the autumn recipes as they are in season and have excellent astringent properties to help cleanse the gut lining. If you prefer to avoid them, please use pears or apples instead.

## Soups

The soup portion size should be half a pint. You will have hopefully made approximately six portions with these recipes so you can freeze for your following week's rebalance days or use as a starter for other mealtimes. Portioning it out in advance will help you stick to the portion size.

If you end up having just half a portion left, you can supplement this by adding some of the stock/potassium broth. This may also help you with the transition to smaller portions.

## Potassium Broth

Maximum of one mug and then drink water afterwards.

## Fruit/Vegetable Drink

For the grated fruit, use about half a pint of the liquid on your rebalance day. It is surprising how little you need. However, if you feel you will need more then you can drink up to one pint of the liquid (you may need three pieces of fruit or vegetables). Freeze any left over for your next rebalance day the following week or use it as part of your normal breakfast the following day. People often end up eating this as a snack or to replace a dessert. This is the benefit of the course: it widens your variety of food and snacks that are healthier and rehydrating.

## Vegetables/leaves

I would use no more than three slices of carrots, or three small broccoli or cauliflower stalks, or the centre of a fennel bulb or half a celery stick. For leaves, I would limit it to two or three fennel leaves and two or three parsley leaves or any other variation. You probably would not want more than this due to the strong taste. These portion sizes are based on organic products which often have a stronger taste and have far more nutrients for their weight. If using non-organic, increase the quantity by up to four times if required.

## Salads

Use a small bowl with just two types of salad one tablespoon of each, and one to two tablespoons quinoa and millet. You may be surprised that you are satisfied with this portion; but remember, if you are hungry still after eating this rebalance salad at lunchtime then **do** have some of your normal lunch food afterwards. The lunchtime meal is when you are most receptive to listening to your body, so if you are still hungry after your salad or protein fix or soup (depending on which season you are in) then have something else – whatever your body tells you to. Try to make it a low GI food so that you are not suddenly raising your blood sugar levels, which will then drop later, causing you to possibly overeat, or eat the wrong food. Sometimes it is just water that your body needs so you may want to try drinking first.

## Final Points

Remember to go over the rescue plan (see Chapter 9). If you get hungry drink water, take light exercise, rest. One of the biggest benefits of the Rebalance Programme is that it regulates the *amount* you eat. You realise it's fresh air, exercise, water and sunlight that your body sometimes really needs rather than food and over time you realise it is about **lifestyle nutrition**!

When you have completed a 24-hour rebalance period it can be an ideal time to introduce sauerkraut into your gut when it has just had a period of clearing out, thereby giving you less of a reaction to these new bacteria if you have a sensitive digestive system. (See 'New to Sauerkraut' in Chapter 9.)

# Autumn Recipes

## *Evening Soup – Pumpkin and Kale*

### *Ingredients*

1 small pumpkin (or butternut squash, sweet potatoes, carrots)

6 kale leaves chopped (stalks removed)

1 onion

1 teaspoon freshly grated ginger (optional)

1 pint of vegetable stock

Sea salt and pepper to taste

### *Method*

I often bake the pumpkin first just to soften it, so it is easier to chop. I usually bake it with whatever I am cooking for the evening meal. If this is not practical, then just chop the pumpkin and remove the seeds and skin as usual but keep them to be used in the stock.

Add the remaining ingredients into a pan and leave to simmer for 1–2 hours on a low heat. Liquidise in a food processor and dilute with vegetable stock to your required consistency.

## *Breakfast – Stewed Pears/Plums and Ginger*

### *Ingredients*

1 small pear or 3 plums

1 teaspoon freshly grated ginger (or ¼ dried ginger) – optional

2–3 tablespoons water

### *Method*

Peel and chop the pear, or if using plums, remove the stones and chop into quarters. Add to a pan with a little water and optional ginger and heat until soft.

You can make a few portions and freeze in small containers in individual servings for convenient use later. This can also be used as a light dessert during the rest of the week.

Although plums are acid forming, I have used them here as they are an excellent fruit to help cleanse the gut lining and are in season during the autumn.

### Morning Soup – Celery and Kale

*Ingredients*

½ whole celery chopped (or fennel or courgettes)

6 large kale leaves with stalks removed

1 onion chopped

1 teaspoon freshly grated ginger (optional)

1 pint of veg stock

Sea salt and pepper to taste

*Method*

Add all the ingredients into a pan and leave to simmer for 1–2 hours on a low heat.

Liquidise in a food processor and dilute with vegetable stock to your required consistency.

If you use a stock with the skin and seeds from the pumpkin this produces a very nurturing soup, not as thin as you might think with the light ingredients. If you find you have an abundance of stock, you can just drink this on its own as it is so tasty with the pumpkin in.

### Mid-Morning Snack

*Ingredients*

1 dessert spoon of pumpkin seeds or 8 almonds

*Method*

Soak the pumpkin seeds in water for 4 hours or overnight in the fridge. If you are having almonds, they need 8 hours to soak so you may want to leave them overnight. Drain off the liquid and enjoy chewing well. You can remove the skins from the almonds if you prefer.

### Alkaline Yog Sub (Yoghurt Substitute)

**Ingredients**

1 dessertspoon creamed coconut (or substitute with desiccated coconut or a vegetable oil)

1 dessertspoon ground almonds

1 teaspoon pumpkin seeds

1 teaspoon linseeds (or ¼ teaspoon chia seeds)

2 dessertspoons cooked quinoa

**Method**

Place all the **dry** ingredients in a jar (excluding the quinoa) and pour in some water until everything is just covered by **2cm**. Leave to soak for 6–12 hours. You can leave it in the fridge for 36 hours. Add the cooked quinoa before enjoying.

# Winter Recipes

The winter soup aims to have a low carbohydrate content and also be green; for example, courgette and pea, kale and broccoli, celery and leek, kale and leek. Use peas as a good *steppingstone to reducing your carbohydrate intake* as they are higher in carbohydrate content than other green vegetables. You could also use just the liquid of a soup you are making, for example, the liquid of sweet potato and kale as another steppingstone.

## *Evening Soup – Courgette and Pea*

### *Ingredients*

3 courgettes chopped (or celery or fennel)

¼ mug frozen peas

1 onion

1 teaspoon freshly grated ginger (optional)

1 pint of vegetable stock

Sea salt and pepper to taste

### *Method*

Add all the ingredients into a pan and leave to simmer for just 1 hour (as the courgettes and peas soften quickly) on a low heat. Liquidise in a food processor and dilute with vegetable stock to your required consistency.

## *Protein Fix*

Serves three rebalance portions or one healthy portion when *not* on your rebalance day.

### *Ingredients*

2 chopped sundried tomatoes soaked overnight (substitute with finely chopped celery carrot or fennel if required)

1 dessertspoon soaked pumpkin seeds (soaking for 4 or 8 hours in fridge)

1 dessertspoon ground almonds (optional or substitute with ground coriander)

1 dessertspoon grated creamed coconut (or any other vegetable oil of your choice)

1 teaspoon linseeds, soaked overnight

¼ carrot peeled and finely chopped or grated

Sea salt and pepper to taste

## *Method*

Drain off the liquid from the soaked items (keeping the sun-dried tomato liquid)

Mix all the ingredients together. Add the liquid of the soaked tomatoes (or water) to produce your desired consistency. Add salt and pepper to taste.

This can be served with vegetable sticks, for example, celery, cucumber or courgette if desired.

## *Grapefruit Juice with Ginger*

Juice *half* a grapefruit and spoon out the remaining flesh and store for later.

Add *freshly* grated or dried ginger to ensure you remain warm.

Ensure the grapefruit is at room temperature when you drink it. Remember if you get cold, your body may start the hunger reflex which you are trying to avoid on your rebalance day.

Use the other half on your next rebalance (this can be frozen once juiced) or eaten later in the week.

**Substitutes for those who have an intolerance to citrus fruits:**

• Hot potassium broth, made from your vegetable stock

• Nettle tea

• If you prefer a fruit drink then you could grate a cooking apple with an eating apple and soak overnight with a quarter teaspoon of fresh ginger. Drain off the liquid and use just half a mug as your rebalance morning drink. This gives a sharper taste like the grapefruit juice.

## *Morning Soup – Leek and Kale*

### *Ingredients*

½ leek chopped (or courgette)

6 large kale leaves with stalks removed

1 onion chopped

1 teaspoon freshly grated ginger

1 pint of vegetable stock

Sea salt and pepper to taste

1 dessertspoon of creamed coconut (optional steppingstone)

### *Method*

Add all the ingredients into a pan and leave to simmer for 1–2 hours on a low heat.

Liquidise in a food processor and dilute with vegetable stock to your required consistency.

# Spring Recipes

The evening soup aims to help you kick start the detox reflex, so it has apples and spices in. If you want to make this a gentler ride, omit the spices.

## *Evening Soup – Sweet Potato and Fenugreek Leaves*

### *Ingredients – serves 6 portions*

3 small sweet potatoes peeled and chopped (or carrots or butternut squash)

Bunch of nettles or kale (or 1 tablespoon dried nettles)

1 onion chopped

1 leek chopped

1 small cooking apple peeled and chopped

1 teaspoon freshly grated ginger (optional)

1 teaspoon freshly grated garlic (optional)

1 teaspoon fenugreek leaves (or a handful of fresh kale)

1 pint of veg stock

Sea salt and cayenne pepper to taste

### *Method*

Add all the ingredients into a pan and leave to simmer for 1 hour or until vegetables are soft. Liquidise in food processor and dilute with vegetable stock to your required consistency. Portion out to small containers for individual servings, half pint per serving. Freeze for future use.

### *Variations*

You can use other root vegetables, for example, butternut squash, parsnips, carrots or celeriac. Avoid normal potatoes as they can be very difficult to digest and, as they belong to the nightshade family, people often suffer from intolerance to them. Most of the root vegetables work well with apples as their sweetness is counterbalanced with the cooking apple. Other spices to use could be turmeric which is particularly useful with its anti-inflammatory properties. Cumin, caraway seeds and coriander also work well. If you cannot get hold of fenugreek leaves, use the seeds instead (soak in water and just use the juice). Leaves are easier to digest than seeds and so are preferred. In my experience fenugreek is the most effective spice to use from the point of view of kickstarting the elimination reflex. Kale can be used instead of fenugreek leaves and can still help your bowels to eliminate.

### Citrus Oil Drink – *makes 2 portions*

#### Ingredients

1 grapefruit juiced

1 lemon juiced

1 orange juiced

2 tablespoons olive oil

Pinch cayenne pepper (optional)

1 teaspoon freshly grated ginger (optional)

1 teaspoon freshly grated garlic (optional)

#### Method

Mix all the ingredients together. Portion out into 2 and freeze if not using immediately. Ensure the juice is at room temperature and stir well when you drink it.

 Other option:

### Stewed Apple and Oil – *serves 3–4 portions (alternative to citrus drink)*

If you have an intolerance to citrus fruits or garlic, use this recipe instead

#### Ingredients

1 cooking apple peeled

1 eating apple peeled

1 tablespoon olive oil

1 teaspoon freshly grated ginger (or half teaspoon dried ginger) – optional

#### Method

Loosely chop the apples and stew together in a little water (with the optional of ginger) until soft. Portion out about 2 tablespoons and add the olive oil. Serve warm.

The apples along with the oil help your liver produce bile which is a vehicle for your body to eliminate toxins. Store remaining stewed apples into individual portions and freeze for the following week.

## Lunchtime Soup – Celery and Nettle

Use non-carbohydrate vegetables to make this a light soup.

**Ingredients** – *serves 6 portions*

1 whole celery chopped (or fennel)

Bunch of nettles or kale

1 onion chopped

1 leek chopped

1 teaspoon freshly grated ginger (optional)

1 pint of vegetable stock

Sea salt and pepper to taste

### Method

Add all the ingredients into a pan and leave to simmer for just 1 hour or until vegetables are soft. Liquidise in food processor and dilute with vegetable stock to your required consistency. Portion out to small containers for individual servings – a half pint per serving. Freeze for future use.

## Potassium Broth – mid-morning snack

See 'General Points for All Seasons' for recipe.

# Summer Recipes

### *Evening Fruit Juice – 2 portions*

#### *Ingredients*

1 apple, 1 pear, grated ginger (optional)

#### *Method*

Peel and grate the pear and apple and place in a large jar. Cover the grated fruit with water and leave for 8 hours at room temperature. This will go brown, but it is still suitable to drink (or eat) later. After the soaking period drain the liquid off and store in a separate jar in the fridge for your evening drink. Ensure it is at room temperature when you drink it unless it is a very hot day. The grated mixture can be used for your breakfast on your normal day or frozen and used at another time. You can add a little ginger or other fruit to bring back some taste if needed when reusing the grated fruit. Elderflowers maybe available to forage so you could just soak 2–3 flower heads instead.

## *Vegetables and Leaves*

A few leaves of two or three varieties are sufficient with a few slices of carrot, or a few slices of the stalks of broccoli or cauliflower.

Ensure you prepare the vegetables and leaves in advance and portion out as you may end up overeating. Try to sit down and chew, swallowing the *liquid only* and discarding the cellulose.

### *Breakfast Fruit Juice – 1–2 portions*

#### *Ingredients*

1 Apple

1 celery stick (or fennel)

grated ginger (optional)

or

¼ cucumber (peeled)

½ fennel bulb

## Method

Grate and peel the apple and the celery stick or cucumber. The celery may be a bit stringy, that is fine; it does not have to be properly grated. Place in a large jar and cover with water and leave for 8 hours at room temperature. The apple will go brown, but it is still suitable to drink (and eat) later. After the soaking period drain the liquid off and store in a separate jar in the fridge for your morning drink. Ensure it is at room temperature when you drink it unless it is really hot weather. You can reuse the grated ingredients for a salad on another day. Add some strong-tasting vegetables or seasoning to enhance the flavour, for example, garlic, onion or cayenne pepper when reusing the grated vegetables on your normal days.

## *Samosa Salad* – 4 portions

### *Ingredients*
Half mug frozen peas
Half mug frozen sweetcorn
Half red pepper chopped finely, or 1 tablespoon chopped sun-dried tomatoes (soaked overnight or grated carrot)
Half small red onion chopped finely or grated (or half small leek)
Dressing:

1 lime, juiced or ½ teaspoon mango powder
1 teaspoon ground cumin
2 teaspoons fenugreek leaves
1 tablespoon sunflower oil or olive oil

### *Method*

Mix dressing in a bowl and then add remaining ingredients and mix well. Portion out into containers suitable for freezing.

## Celery and Apple Salad – 12 portions

### Ingredients

4 sticks of celery chopped finely (can substitute with fennel)

2 tablespoons of stewed apple (1 cooking apple and 1 eating apple)

Grated leek (2cm of the white stalk)

1 dessertspoon ground almonds

1 tablespoon olive oil

1 teaspoon cider vinegar

1 dessertspoon of dried nettles (or any herb of your choice, fresh or dried)

1 dessertspoon pumpkin seeds (optional) – soak in water for 4 hours

Sea salt and pepper to taste

### Advanced Preparation

1. Soak the pumpkin seeds in water for 4 hours (or leave in the fridge overnight and drain off in the morning)

2. Peel and chop the apples and place in a pan with a *little* water to start stewing. Heat until the apples can be mashed into a stiff paste. The trick is to only use a little water. Use one cooking and one eating apple for maximum flavour and texture. Leave to cool before adding to the celery.

### Method

Grate the leek and mix with the stewed apple, oil, vinegar, ground almonds, herbs and seasoning.

Add in the chopped celery and *drained* pumpkin seeds.

Stir well and store in the fridge for up to 3 days. Or freeze in small portions for quick defrosting and convenience.

### Quinoa and Millet Mix – 8 portions – to go with your salad

#### Ingredients

⅕ cup millet grain (or substitute with quinoa)

⅘ cup quinoa

2 cups of water

#### Method

1. Put the dry grain into a pan and rinse in cold water. Drain using a sieve and return to the pan.

2. Add the water and leave to soak overnight. The next day simmer for 25 minutes with a *lid on*. Leave for a further 10 minutes *off* the heat *still* with the lid *on* so the moisture is fully absorbed.

### Potassium Broth (see 'General Points for All Seasons')

*Alternative to Potassium Broth* If you prefer a cool drink at this time of year or an easier drink to prepare, then you can use very low GI foods such as celery, cucumber, under ripe pears or fennel. Use the grating method described above. Add ginger if you need to 'warm it up'.

# Sauerkraut Recipe

Although this can be bought from health food shops and some supermarkets, you get different strains of bacteria when you make it yourself. Also, you are reducing the packaging impact on the environment. Once you get confident you can also make your own flavours, mixing red and white cabbage produces a lovely pink colour and a slightly different taste, or add other vegetables such as carrot or onion.

## *Ingredients*

1 large cabbage

Sea salt, about 1 teaspoon (optional)

The salt draws the water out of the cabbage and creates the brine in which it ferments and prevents cabbage from rotting. Sea salt has lots of essential minerals so please do feel *good* about the salt, and it helps the brine to come out of the cabbage. You can omit it and it will still ferment; you just need to ensure you have liquid coming out of the cabbage by mixing and pressing well.

## *Method*

Remove *outer* leaves and cut the *end* stalk off. Then grate the cabbage, including the stalked centre of the cabbage as this has much of the nutrients.

Mix in a big bowl, adding salt.

Slowly add into a large, sterilised jar and press down with a spoon as you go. The pressing helps create the brine. Make sure the jar is full, with about 1 inch (2.5cm) space to the top for the expansion due to fermentation. If the jar is under full, the sauerkraut is at risk of going off. Better to over fill rather than under fill.

Once the brine starts to come out, seal with a tight lid. Store on a plate, or tray, on the kitchen surface (just in case the brine overflows from the jar) and away from direct sunlight and other heat sources. Press the cabbage down with a spoon twice each day for 3–5 days.

After 2 to 3 days it starts to ferment, and you get the added benefit of good bacteria. If the brine is oozing out of the jar, take some out and push down again with a spoon to ensure there is liquid brine at the top. If it starts to dry out add some cooled, sterilised, salted water.

After about a week, it is ready to eat; the longer you leave it fermenting the more bacteria is created.

Store in or out of the fridge. Sauerkraut made this way will keep for at least 2 months. The longer you keep it, the stronger the taste and quantity of bacteria. See 'New to Sauerkraut' in Chapter 9.

**Variation**

If you have an intolerance to cabbage, you may still be OK with it fermented provided you follow the 'New to Sauerkraut' guide. However, some people still have an intolerance to fermented cabbage or just don't like the taste, so I suggest using carrots instead. Follow the same recipe as above and you may need to finely grate the carrot to create a brine; experiment with your own grater or food processor to find the best texture for you.

# Embracing a New Approach to Food – Finding Your Way to Optimal Health

Embracing this new approach to food may be a bit tricky to start with, but over time when you apply it repeatedly for just 24 hours once a week you can start to find your way to optimal health. This is not a static place. We change over time, not just with the seasons but in our phases in life. Being able to stop and rest your digestion helps you anchor yourself through theses changes and makes the transitions easier.

You have done so well already by getting this far through the book. Have you done your first rebalance? Do you find you lose it and then it's always tricky to get back into it? Or have you established a routine that works for you and are happy with your health? Or maybe you would like to take it a step further? Wherever you are, would you like some more help with this? As you have got this far, I have an exclusive offer that may be beneficial for you...read on.

# Exclusive Offer

I would love you to get the most out of this book, and so to supplement the great content contained in these pages I have some additional material and support organised online for you.

Visit www.integratinghealth.com/booksupport to access this free audio recording and a free book support session worth over £150.00.

I wrote this book to help you live your life to the full. Follow this link now and let's make that happen together:

www.integratinghealth.com/offer.

# About The Author

I live and work in the Lake District with my two sons. As a child, I had digestive problems which hindered my true dream to be a dancer. I loved cooking and started to create my own recipes that worked for me. These have been passed on to friends and clients via bits of paper and eventually books. I now follow my passion and teach slow flow yoga, nearly a dancer! With my love of the great outdoors, I also teach outside in parks and woodlands. I now combine these two passions: food and movement on yoga retreats in the Lake District.

Printed in Great Britain
by Amazon